AN ACCIDENTAL
GURU

A Universal Guide to Happy
in Layman's Terms

JAKE TYSON

BALBOA.PRESS
A DIVISION OF HAY HOUSE

Balboa Press books may be ordered through booksellers or by contacting:

Balboa Press
A Division of Hay House
1663 Liberty Drive
Bloomington, IN 47403
www.balboapress.com.au
AU TFN: 1 800 844 925 (Toll Free inside Australia)
AU Local: 0283 107 086 (+61 2 8310 7086 from outside Australia)

Because of the dynamic nature of the Internet, any web addresses or
links contained in this book may have changed since publication and
may no longer be valid. The views expressed in this work are solely those
of the author and do not necessarily reflect the views of the publisher,
and the publisher hereby disclaims any responsibility for them.

The author of this book does not dispense medical advice or prescribe the use
of any technique as a form of treatment for physical, emotional, or medical
problems without the advice of a physician, either directly or indirectly. The
intent of the author is only to offer information of a general nature to help
you in your quest for emotional and spiritual well-being. In the event you use
any of the information in this book for yourself, which is your constitutional
right, the author and the publisher assume no responsibility for your actions.

Print information available on the last page.

ISBN: 978-1-5043-1510-4 (sc)
ISBN: 978-1-5043-1511-1 (e)

Balboa Press rev. date: 07/15/2020

Life, a thought

Existing Together

Imagine eight billion movie cinemas, and eight billion totally different movies, all playing at the same time.

That's us.

Each one of us is inventing our own movie. We are the director and lead actor of our movie. Everyone else is our cast, but you and I all play supporting roles, extras, for each other's movies.

We all live on the same planet, but we all live in billions of different worlds, and those worlds are of our own making.

Truth.

CONTENTS

ACKNOWLEDGEMENTS

To my family and friends, the Universe/God, Paramahansa Yogananda.

Thank you.

FOREWORD

Jake Tyson was a beer-drinking, durry-smoking, potty-mouthed and depressed tradesman who one night found himself standing on a northern beaches cliff top, just a step away from ending his own life.

This then atheist single father asked 'god knows what' for answers in one last ditch attempt to rise above his monstrous emotional pain. To his surprise, the answers actually came.

Over the next 24 months he allowed "the voice" to flow through him and out onto the page, until eventually, he had penned The Universal Guide to Happiness.

This beautiful book invites the reader to own the truth of who they are (love), to respect oneself deeply (no matter who or what has come before) and to use the power of their heart and imagination to step into a more deeply honorable and enjoyable experience of self in this life.

Incidentally, many of the concepts channelled are now supported by neuroscience, epigenetics and metaphysics... which brings me to my last point.

One of the most extraordinary things about this book is it's unlikely messenger. Jake didn't bury himself in textbooks to access the information shared.

While he admits he is still very far from perfect, by

allowing a higher truth to move through him and aligning himself to it, he is now living a meaningful life he loves and is helping others through the power of his story.

Eloise King
Journalist & Creator of *The Self-Love Project*
<u>www.theselfloveproject.com</u>

PROLOGUE

My eleventh hour

So, here I am. On top of a headland, sobbing like a baby. Broken, pissed and devastated. My partner, my beautiful partner, mother of our one-year old daughter, has just walked out on me. I can't pay rent. I have no money. I'm drinking all the time. I smoke and take drugs and act like a shit.

I'm so fed up. Fed up with myself, my crappy life, the same stupid mistakes I keep making and making. I meet and fall in love with amazing women, then ruin the relationship till they leave me. I love my children so much, my three amazing kids, but my family life, and life in general, is a mess. I work hard, create great businesses, and let them fail. I'm sick of myself, my fucked-up life, even sick of the excuses I tell myself.

Tears run from my eyes. I have snot all over my face. I am a mess. I crack another beer. I'm thinking it'll be my last. I neck it, trying to escape my own head. I'm ready to end it all. This cliff is high enough to do the job. But I'm desperate for answers, for another solution.

I stand up, staggering. I am alone and lost. My last scraps of resolve and emotion gather inside me and form my final call. "God, fucking help me. What do I do?" I surrender. I'm done. Spent.

The last thing I expected was an answer. But answers were

coming, as clear as if someone was sitting right next to me. And it was sudden, an understanding delivered in an instant. All at once, I was in a conversation with someone, something – and it was talking right to me, talking me back off that cliff, talking me back to my life.

I'm not a religious man. I'm not even particularly spiritual. I'm just a bloke whose life was falling apart, at my most vulnerable and exposed, standing on a cliff, begging for help. And, incredibly, help and guidance is what I got. Without any judgement, just plain and simple and practical. Understanding, knowing, and a love I never knew or felt before. It was like I'd been slapped across the face and woken up.

Suddenly, I realised I had been searching for some kind of spirituality, consciousness, or God, my whole life. Funny thing is, I had been getting answers like this the whole time, I'd just been ignoring them. Now, I had that feeling you get when you're looking tirelessly for your car keys and finally realise, hey, they've been in my hand the whole time.

This incredible love, understanding and guidance had always been there, I just was completely unaware of it.

Where did it come from? God, Source, the Universe, whatever you want to call it, it's all the same thing. I like to call God the Universe. I sat on that cliff for hours, getting answers to every single question I asked. Weird, right? But also, pretty bloody cool.

That night, my life changed course. How could it not? I went from wanting to jump off a cliff to wanting and understanding life. The experience I had, and continue to have, has completely altered the way I think, the way I experience my life, the way I think about and treat other people, and how I feel. I/we are separate to nothing. We are all part of the "one" consciousness.

But you know what? I'm not special. I'm really not. I'm just a regular dude, a bit rough around the edges, who definitely swears too much. I'm probably the least likely guy you would expect to have a spiritual experience on top of a cliff in the middle of the night. I certainly never thought that could or would ever happen to me!

But it did, and what I've learned, I have to share. It's too good not to.

This book, *The Universal Guide to Happiness*, is what I was shown that night, and over time since. It's simple, gets straight to the point, and will help you to find your own happiness as soon as possible.

It won't tell you what to think. But it will help us understand why we experience what we do, help us stop experiencing what we no longer want, and how to consciously attain what we *do* want, such as love, happiness, being one, or more worldly goals, like financial security.

We all have this ability and can tap into it anytime we want. Anyone can do it. You don't need any equipment, and it won't cost you any money. You already have everything you need. Happiness is actually found within you. This guide will help you find out how.

None of this is meant to be hard, and truthfully, it's not. Honestly, it won't be for everyone. That's OK. But for others, it'll be everything they've been looking for.

Anyhow, let's get to the good stuff. Try and be open and not overthink what you read. Go with it, and it will come together.

Peace,

Jake

So, what are we really talking about here?

A while later, the Universe asked me to write this guide. I said, 'I'm no guru or preacher. I'm sitting here with a beer and cigarette in my hand while I talk to you. I spent my fifteen minutes of fame on TV, mostly hungover. I yahooed around drunk on my motorcycle, and lost my knee doing it. I've ruined relationships and friendships. I've made money and lost it. I've fucked up so many times, why would you want *me* to write this guide"?

The reply the Universe gave me was clear as day and said, 'Well Jake, why *not* you? Think about it. You haven't *really* messed up, because everything you've ever done has led you here. Sure, you've kicked a few bad habits, and you're still growing every day, and yes, far from perfect. *That's* why you're the perfect person to write this guide. If *you* can do this, anyone can. You asked me for it. Write it like you're talking to one of your friends in the pub, just less some of the bad language".

I'm still working on the swearing, but I get where this message is coming from.

I failed English at school and have never written a thing, so the good news is, no big words are used in this guide.

And body conscious – yep been there. I hid my mangled leg from everyone for nearly 20 years. Even in bed with my partners. I thought all I was, was my body. I played the blame game and cried 'why me' for years, but that's over now. I have three awesome kids I'm grateful for, and losing my knee was a gift. I wouldn't change a thing. We can't change the past anyway! But we can change our futures. This guide will show us that.

There is a lot of information out there now about spirituality and consciousness, and much of it seems exclusive, or airy-fairy, or draped in crystals and tie-dye. Consciousness could easily be mistaken for something that can only be acquired by a special few. This is not true. And you don't have to sit in lotus position for three hours a day to achieve it. It's not all seriousness. One thing all great spiritual gurus have in common is a great sense of humor.

Consciousness starts with awareness, and that is our direct connection to God/the Universe. All we must do is remember this or be reminded of it. That's what *The Universal Guide to Happy* is about - awareness. With it, we can create and invent happy for the rest of our lives, from this day on.

There's no judgment here, but there is a universal law, nature's law, that we can't escape. It's a cycle, or a wheel as Buddhists put it. Everything we do rolls around and catches up on us. I call it thought inventing. We may be able to fool other people, even ourselves, but we cannot fool the Universe. I am living proof with the shit fight I invented for myself in the past. Yes, I invented it! But the great news is, we can change it if we want to.

We are our thoughts and this guide will help us become

aware of that. Then, we can consciously invent our future experiences. We can take control of our own thoughts and be aware of what we are inventing right now. True happiness is peace. A life spent laughing no matter what.

We all chose to be here on Earth, and our soul has its own purpose that it wants to experience. But we need to get back to some of the basics, because we are leaving some great things behind. Like love and compassion for one another, community and the spirit. We are all in this together, and we are all part of the one universe. This doesn't mean we all have to start singing Kumbaya. It means gaining an awareness of who we really are.

I will use my own life experiences as an example from time to time. Relationships, childhood, adult life and so on - it'll roll out as we get into it. But this isn't all about me, it's about us. All of us.

This guide explains the Universal laws that invent and create our lives here on Earth. These principles are laid out clearly and simply, and each chapter finishes with at least one example of using the Universal guides, so we can all start straight away. Its what I asked the Universe for, "how does this work'?!

In the last third of this guide, the Universe answers some awesome questions I had about life. But firstly, I needed to be conscious about how, and why.

There's a glossary at the back that explains some of the common words used throughout the guide. Refer to it anytime you need to.

Thank you for being a part of this. Happy days ahead!

Life, a thought

Swimming with the riptide

Pushing against our souls' purpose is like swimming against a riptide at the beach. It's tiring and we go nowhere. This is what it's like living in the mind.

When we go with the riptide, it is so much easier. Then we just veer off to the left or right and our truth takes us where we need to go.

The Universe knows what it's doing and can't be sped up. It's like trying to rotate Earth quicker than it's meant to go. We cannot speed up morning to night.

Imagine, think and talk about everything we consciously want and want to be, then just sit back in it. Enjoy it and know that it's coming. That's the fun part.

DEFINITIONS

Mind

Ego, anger, fear, worry, hate, judgement, disappointment, pain, sorrow, blame. The mind is like being the only horse in a race that never ends. The mind is constantly lying to us and who we 'think' we are is not who we really are. Otherwise known as ego. Our mind is always lurking around. Free will allows us to pick, mind or truth. Mind is part of the brain. The brain is basically an advanced computer and fantastic storage unit that helps calculate things through our senses. But like a computer, the brain is constantly getting viruses. Believing everything we see and hear is not our Truth.

Truth

Love, consciousness, awareness, happiness, passion, openness, lack of judgment, soul's journey, forgiveness, compassion, our personal radar. Love for everyone, or even our favourite hobbies like playing an instrument. Truth is the only consistent emotion that ever feels good.

CHAPTER 1

THOUGHT ENERGY EMOTION – CHANGED IN A SPLIT SECOND

From the age of about fifteen to twenty-one, I suffered with extreme depression. Depression is real, I've lived it and nearly ended myself over it. It requires a hell of a lot of energy. They call depression being flat line, and not being able to feel, but you actually feel a hell of a lot, and most of it is negative. Fear, blame, guilt, shame, anger, loss of control, hopelessness.

I was living hell in my mind, every hour of every day. It was like being in a deep, deep hole, with no way of getting out, and a heavy sky above pressing down on me. I was being buried alive, every hour of every day. My mind was living me, and I was utterly self-consumed.

I also suffered with hypochondria and was at the doctor every other day for a blood test, or with some weird ailment that didn't exist. I thought I was dying but the fear of dying was killing me, so I was trying to save myself before I died.

No doctor could help me. My thoughts actually had me believing I had brain tumours, liver disease - pretty much every illness under the sun. I could actually feel pain that didn't exist, but I made that pain exist through my thought. I was searching for reasons to feel like shit. Thought energy with strong emotion held onto for long enough invents our experience, and that's exactly what I was doing.

MY FIRST GIFT

So here I am, age 21, living my mind. I want out of my mind and my thoughts. I am drinking, doing drugs and riding my motor bike like I'm in some kind of Grand Prix. Trying to kill myself, without actually having to do it myself. Something had to give.

I thought it would be death and out of this life here on Earth. Turns out it wasn't my time. One moment I'm flying along, high as can be, the next I'm on the side of the road, my leg torn off from above my knee. I had collided with a car. I lay on the side of the road, feeling a smashing pain in my skull as the blood pumps out of my leg.

The pain is appalling, otherworldly. I really do think I am going to die. And I suddenly know it is not *at all* what I want. "God," I cry, "please don't let me die".

It is here that I have my first connection with the Universe.

"Jake, you are not going to die".

Instantly, I am calm. Today isn't my day to die. I know it, know it is absolutely true.

As intense and profound as this was, I would dismiss this connection with the Universe for another 20 years. I convinced myself I had made it all up in my mind.

I wake up in hospital, in what would be my home for a while. All these pins are coming out of my leg, or what used to look like a leg. Now it's like something out of an abattoir. I am in real physical trouble here. Suddenly, I know I need to get on with shit. Now I *really am* sick!

I instantly forget all my past mind troubles and focus on getting better. Looking back now, I realise I didn't even consciously know I was doing it. I concentrated on looking healthy and strong and getting myself out of hospital. My emotion was only on what I wanted to *be*, not on what I didn't want. I was already fucked, and I didn't want or need more of that.

I wanted my health. I wanted life. My first goal was to get out of my hospital bed and go for a pee on my own. I did this after seven weeks. I remember being so happy and grateful for that. Not once did I care about how much money I had, if I still had a job, what car I had or what was on TV. Judgement and worrying about what others were doing was gone. My brain tumours, liver disease, ringing in the ears and all the bullshit illnesses I made up in my mind were gone. Worrying about what other people thought of me, or didn't think of me became obsolete, not even a thought.

SO, WHAT CHANGED (APART FROM LOSING A KNEE DOWN THE GUTTER)?

Only one thing changed. My vibration. What changed my vibration? My thought. Who I AM. I realise now, I was who I thought I was, but I wasn't. I was living past conditioning, shit that didn't belong to me, other people's rights and wrongs and judgements that were not mine. We can end up living past conditionings that can happen when we are children. I was living others' lives and their thoughts, that I had allowed to become mine. I had allowed myself to be programmed because I had forgotten my truth.

Don't get me wrong. We don't need to have our legs torn off to change our thoughts. This really isn't rocket science.

Physical pain is nothing. Thought energy of the mind is

hell! But it is only our thought energy vibration that needs to be tweaked. Like getting a car tuned. We get our vibration idling right first, bit by bit. Then follow the Universal Guide to Happy principles. Thought energy with our truth and remembering who we really are is bliss.

That experience feels like it was yesterday. I can laugh now because it doesn't belong to me anymore. I was living my mind at the time. The thing is, it was real, or at least that's what I let my mind believe.

It would still take me another 20 years of pain, being an arsehole, and my "cliff" experience with God/Universe, to consciously understand what I was doing. I can truthfully say, I don't think I'd be alive now if my motorcycle accident hadn't slowed me down. My leg being torn off was a gift. It sent me on a different path. Without it I probably wouldn't have got this guide. It was meant to be and is part of my soul's journey.

THOUGHT INVENTING

Remember the scene in Star Wars, the first one where the droid R2D2 shoots out the laser beam that creates the hologram of Princess Leia saying, "Help me Obi-Wan Kenobi, you're my only hope." This is exactly what we are doing with our thoughts. They are the beam, and our emotion, depending on its strength, creates the hologram. The hologram symbolises our physical manifestation and life experience that we are inventing with our thoughts and emotion.

So, the first thing we must become aware of is that our thoughts invent everything that we experience. When we realise our thoughts invent everything, we are immediately conscious and start to wake up. Get through this first chapter and there will be lights flicking on everywhere, and it gets really easy.

From a very early age we know what the wind is. It's so second nature to know. None of us have ever seen it, but we absolutely know that the wind exists. We see how it moves the leaves on a tree or fills a yacht's sail to push it through the water. We feel it on our face. Although wind itself is invisible, we have no doubt about its energy.

Sound too is invisible, energy that vibrates in such a way that our ears can sense it, pick it up and process it. But we can't see sound. You've seen the clips of sound or water on top of a speaker cone, rippling and moving in waves? This is a visual of how that sound is vibrating, another version of what we hear with our ears. But we can't see the sound.

In fact, what we *can* see is not even a drop in the ocean of what really exists.

It's nothing new to know that we humans – and every other solid thing we see - are made up of 99.9% empty space. We get taught it in high school physics, when we're learning mass and density. Everything is made of atoms, and atoms are mostly empty space.

Our bodies are actually like the silk parts of a spider's web. If all the empty space between all our cells was taken away and we were compressed, we would be no larger than a pea. Our size is just an illusion of what really is.

So, if we are nearly all empty space, what are we?

We are vibrating energy and thought.

Our thoughts are as real as the wind. We know they are there and can see a product of what they invent. And in fact, our thoughts invent our experiences. Whatever it is we think about, we attract, and then experience in our physical life. But, there must be emotion behind it and that emotion must have passion. Is the emotion positive or negative? Awareness is the key.

Example of Empty Space

The body looks larger to the eye than it is. It's the emptiness between that makes us anything. What we can't see, is everything. Vibrating Energy.

The Body

Vibrating Energy, Empty Space. What we are.

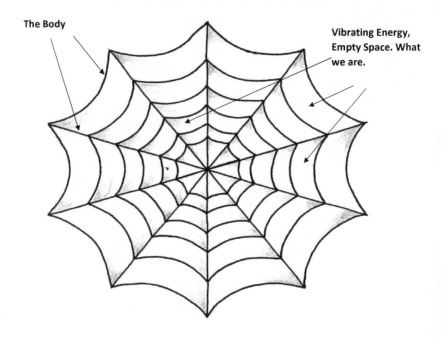

This is thought energy, and with it you can invent the experiences you want to have and stop having the ones you don't.

No one is taught about thought energy at school, and its most important subject in life. My parents certainly didn't teach me about it. But, that's because they didn't know. I lived nearly forty years oblivious to the power of thought energy and how real it is. I lived in my mind, with my negative and judgemental thoughts, and had no idea they were inventing my life experiences.

THOUGHT ENERGY 80-20 RULE

Often, we focus our thoughts on exactly what we *don't* want. Mostly we aren't even conscious of it. Our minds are judgemental and like to create fear and worry. If we give enough thought energy and emotion to something for long enough, positive or negative, we draw that experience closer to ourselves. The more we worry and think about what we don't have, what's going wrong and so on, the more of that we are inventing. Frustration is a perfect example.

So, we need to apply the 80-20 rule. We need to be conscious and focus at least 80% of our thought energy on what we do want (and not dwell on what we don't). If we want to be wealthy but only think 20% positive thoughts on wealth, and the other 80% goes on how poor we are, and lack of wealth, we are going to remain poor.

We need to be aware of how we are thinking and turn our thought emotion around the second we catch ourselves slipping into the negative emotion.

If we want to be fit and healthy or lose weight, we must picture ourselves as strong, fit and lean. We need to talk about it with emotion and hold on to it, create the positive image and see ourselves there at our goal. Eventually, we will get there. Our thoughts with emotion invent it, it's a Universal promise.

NEGATIVE THOUGHT ENERGY IN RELATIONSHIPS

A friend of mine was constantly entering her relationships thinking that her partner was going to have an affair or run off with someone else. She would focus so much attention on it. It was often without merit and she was basing her fear on a past experience with an ex-partner.

She was entering all her relationships in this fear-based thought. This thought and worry had her mind so wrapped up she would eventually voice it to her partner or accuse them of something that had not happened. Sure enough, the relationship would end again, exactly as all her previous ones had.

Then she'd say, "I knew that would happen, I just knew it"! She had some "fuck you" vindication emotion behind that statement too.

A verbalised thought with passion and strong emotion, held onto for long enough, has incredible power and energy. Or thoughts, repeated and spoken about enough times, can invent anything.

Did *she* have the affair? No. But did her thoughts and words perhaps have a play in the outcome? Did her verbalised thoughts and fear create something that once didn't exist? Maybe a seed was planted and spoken enough times to her partner, and it grew.

Many relationships start off with passion. We are both giving great thought energy to each other. Once we start focusing on what's not happening, or what they do that shits us to tears, and stick with those thoughts for long enough, that's what we get more of. And relationships end. Our vibration changes and no longer matches theirs. Regardless, if we look for the negative in the most perfect flower in the world, we will find it.

POSITIVE THOUGHT ENERGY
IN RELATIONSHIPS

My friend ended up breaking the cycle and has been very happily in love for some time now. She doesn't worry about things that haven't happened because she doesn't want that. She focuses her thought energy on what she wants. She decided to love and trust. Her thoughts on her partner are far more positive than negative, and she gets her thoughts back in return. The rest just is. Swim with the riptide and only give thought to positive things we want. If it's with love and wanting to see others happy, it feels great too. That's our truth.

GIVE IT TIME

With every thought there is space, a time delay in bringing it to life. This is the Universe's way of making sure we really do want it. We need to be persistent.

Some of us reading this now have been on diets and training programs to lose weight. Often after three weeks we chuck in the towel. The mind is impatient, hasn't seen the results and wants to give in. It tugs at our willpower and tries to pull us back to our old habits. When this happens, the positive thought energy and emotion can die. Our mind thrives off being disappointed.

My mind was no different. I'll use money as an example. I asked the Universe why I had been broke for so long, why I was always so hard up for money and why it was so damn hard to make my business a success? The answer I got was, "What Jake, you didn't want that? It's what you focused so much of your thought energy on for months, even years, with emotion. You spoke about all these things with passion. Many times a day, to many different people!"

Turns out the Universe was right. Whenever I'd made a little bit of money, I'd spend 80% of my thought energy on the fear and worry of not having it anymore or losing it, instead of focusing on being grateful for my achievement and planning how to be strategic and focus on it growing. Guess what I got? Exactly what I thought and worried about. Yep, I lost it. My thought energy of the mind had me focusing on what I did and didn't have. I got more loneliness, more anger, less money, more depressed and more shit. I asked for it and got it every time. The Universe always delivers to us our thoughts and what we hold on to with emotion. Positive or negative to us at the time.

But it doesn't have to be like this. Reach for your original thought with emotion, love, passion and excitement. If we keep talking about, and picturing ourselves who we want to be, doing the things we want to do, we will become this. We can absolutely expect it. Accept it, it's the Universal law. If you want to be strong and healthy, picture yourself loving exercise, enjoying healthy food and making good choices. It's never a diet that works, it's the thought energy and emotion of the person behind it. And the only difference between what we label "lucky" and "unlucky" people, is their thoughts.

Allowing our thoughts time to become reality can also save us pain. Another word for time is space – we've all said, "just give me a bit of space". This is exactly what our thoughts need too.

When we are conscious, even non-conscious, the space gap gives us a chance to change our thought that may have not been a good idea in the first place. How often do we find ourselves saying, "I thought I wanted that, but I actually didn't"? How many teenagers at times of anger have wished their parents dead? Wow, lucky that thought doesn't come into play immediately! Two minutes later they'd be sobbing and saying, "I never wanted that"! And I personally would have died a few times by now.

Think any thought we want with truth emotion, then we are on the right track. Remember, truth is love. Love is an emotion and passion for someone or something, like playing a musical instrument. No matter what, this emotion always makes you feel great.

HOW DO WE START TO CHANGE OUR THOUGHTS?

Throw worry and fear away forever. They don't help one bit.

"Consciously" talk about what you really do want, all the time. Day dream about what you want or want to be, what inspires you, fantasise. Pick a few little things to start off, so you can consciously notice them come to life: "I am happy. I am relaxed. I love my work." Whatever it is you want. Then go as large as you want! Write it down and read it back to yourself aloud every day as many times as you can. Keep adding to it and reading it back to yourself, aloud. Back the thought energy with passion and emotion. Add as much emotion as possible. Live it right NOW, like it's already happening.

Put your thought energy vibration out there and you will draw the people you need into your life to make it happen. It will happen, it always does. Hold onto it and don't even worry about how it will happen, the Universe takes care of this for us. Every time!

THOUGHT ENERGY + EMOTION
+ SPOKEN WORD (SOUND)

We all know that sounds are vibrating energy. A thought sounded and verbalised has a million times more power than a thought just on its own. That's the start of a thought being actioned. This, with strong emotion behind it, can invent anything - any experience we want (or don't want if we're worrying about it enough). Putting thought to anything we don't want, don't have or fear happening, is insane.

Gandhi, Buddha, Jesus, Paramahansa Yogananda and many other prophets and gurus knew the power of thought energy and spoken word. Their words were spoken with such truth, such emotion, that they live on forever. Buddha never voiced an opinion of someone else or uttered a spoken word that he did not want to experience. He was conscious of the power of thought energy and a spoken word. It becomes part of us. If we don't want to experience something, don't say it.

Many other well-known identities — Einstein, Bill Gates, Steve Jobs, Martin Luther King, Winston Churchill, Anthony Robbins, Oprah Winfrey — all use thought energy plus emotion plus spoken word (sound).

Every single one of these people had a thought energy with such strong emotion, they *had* to share it with others and talk about it all the time.

It always involves others. Success is a collective effort. It's Universal!

Onto the good stuff, here it is! The evidence thought energy is as real as you are reading this now.

Life, a thought

The life dream

The only difference between a dream and what we label "reality" is – remembering. If we couldn't remember yesterday or the day before, today is no different to a dream. Live the dream!

CHAPTER 2

SPOKEN WORD INVENTS

THOUGHT, SPOKEN WORD, INVENTS

Without thought, nothing in this Universe would have been invented or exist. But without emotion, thought stops. Emotion is what brings a thought to life and into the physical experience. The power of thought is one of life's most important and powerful inventions.

A spoken word is a sound that comes out of our mouth.

A sound is absolute vibrating energy, the same as us.

A spoken word with emotion and passion, equals vibrating energy, which started as thought.

Once thought energy with strong emotion becomes a spoken word, it's then sound. That sound creates a certain vibration. Like a high note or low note on a piano, no different. Keep making that sound and holding that thought with emotion, and those sounds become powerful vibrating thought energy waves, cast out to the Universe.

These thoughts will soon come back to us as reality, for

us to experience. It's absolute. By thinking about what you want, and using your voice to create sound, you are inventing an image of what you want to experience, and this image will soon become your life experience.

Be aware - by focusing on what you don't want, or what's not happening, or fear, we get that same thing back.

When I was a teenager, my father would play the piano on Saturday afternoons. From my bedroom, I would hear him play. He would always stick to the same songs and play ones he loved. I could tell from the sound and vibration coming from the piano exactly what he was feeling. Without seeing or speaking to him, I would know if it was a good time to ask him for a loan of fifty dollars. I knew exactly his thought and emotion from the vibration he sent out through the piano if the answer would be yes or no.

Our thought strength depends on the emotion behind our spoken word, just like the vibration sent out through Dad's piano depended on his emotion at the time. The vibrating energy of sound, voiced with passion and belief, is unstoppable. It hits every target, every time. It's absolute. The Universe gives us what we focus thought energy on. Being aware is key. Are you speaking with your truth, or with your mind?

It's so simple. Prove it to yourself now. Pick an experience from your past. What were your thoughts at the time? How were you thinking and speaking about other people? Or about yourself? Did those thoughts, and the way you were talking, invent an experience for you, months, or years after that? Personally, for years I was inventing more and more of the same old shit and I had no idea I was even doing it.

But it is possible to change the course of our experiences, simply by imagining what it is we want to experience, feeling that desire, and putting our voice to it.

THOUGHT ENERGY AND
MATCHING VIBRATION

What's your favourite song right now? How does it make you feel? When you hear that song, you feel its vibration, and that vibration that matches yours. Something about that song creates a thought, and that triggers an emotion. That powerful emotion then invents an experience for you.

When our thought energy vibration matches something or someone else's vibration, we experience them, and see them in our physical life. Everyone we see, from the strangers in the street to the lovers in our bed, match our thought energy vibration in some way.

Imagine our thought vibrations as millions of search lights sweeping the night sky. When our thought vibrations cross with another's matching thought vibrations, they are locked in, and then presented to us in physical life.

It's important to add that if our thought energy vibration doesn't match something or someone else's, we won't be seen, and we won't experience it. No different to the wind. We are there, but invisible.

FOR INSTANCE, …

Anthony Robbins is a popular speaker. I personally don't know much about him or his teachings, but I do know the Universal vibration he is using. When Anthony is on stage, he speaks with super-powerful emotion. That emotion comes from his thought energy.

It's not the words that come out of Anthony's mouth that inspire people. It's the sound, the vibration of the sound, and the powerful emotion behind the sound that connects with those in his audiences' vibrations and elevates them. Their passionate thought already wanted it and they are ready to be inspired, well before Anthony even opens his mouth. Their thought energy with strong emotion is there to receive it. Their vibration is already matching Anthony's.

Anthony's thought energy plus strong emotion, passion, and want for others' happiness, creates the spoken word and vibration. Anthony's spoken word is then picked up, by millions of people, who think about and speak about Anthony's words with emotion.

What was once just Anthony's thought, is now global. Anthony thought it. Anthony spoke it with emotion and invented it. Anthony invented his own world with thought.

It's now obvious, right? Thought *is* vibrating energy, just like the wind. But we need to be aware of our thoughts and focus our thoughts on what we want. Remember the 80 – 20 rule? What we don't want to exist, we mustn't give thought to. We certainly don't talk about it and give it energy and life. If we don't give it any thought, its energy stops, and it basically dies.

Buddha and Jesus's words for example, live on, and always will. Their truth, with love, happiness and spoken word, is thought about and spoken by hundreds of millions of people a day. Their thought energy will never stop.

Our thoughts and spoken word invent our thought energy and vibration. Make sure your thoughts are positive and hold onto them with passion, emotion and love. Sound out your thoughts with emotion for long enough, and you will experience it.

Our thoughts are just like the laser that creates a 4D hologram. We are constantly inventing our physical life with our thought energy, every day.

Our Thoughts are our Virtual Reality

Remember the R2D2 analogy? Our life inventing is like looking through Virtual Reality goggles. We can move left, move right, look around and even lose our balance. However, there is no fear because we remember what we are doing, and the game is just a programme.

Life, (our eyes), is our personal reality inventing to our **thoughts**. Our **Thoughts** are programming every single experience in our life. Our thoughts with emotion create the beam that then presents its self in physical life to us. What are our thoughts? Money, new car, house, holiday, love, family = imagination, thought.

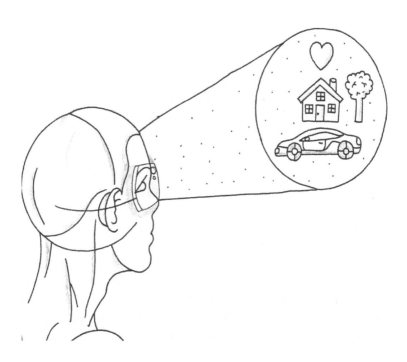

WE ARE AN OPEN BOOK TO OTHERS

If we want to see what someone thinks of themselves, all we need to do is watch how they talk about other people and the world around them.

Our opinions and how we talk about other people and certain situations are an exact reflection of ourselves. We own our thoughts, we *are* our thoughts. Our thoughts are us, no-one else. Being conscious of the thought energy we project out to the Universe with our emotion and spoken words is important, because our thoughts are coming to meet us.

Being conscious of our thoughts takes a little practice, but soon it becomes second nature, like getting fit or even going to sleep.

CHAPTER 3

SEPARATE FROM NOTHING

BEING CONSCIOUS OF OUR THOUGHTS

Most of the time, our thoughts are in our minds. This is where the day to day happens – what's for dinner, what will I wear, I must mow the lawn, god I'm getting fat, I have no money. That kind of thing. It's also known as our ego.

The trouble with our minds is that it's really easy to get stuck inside them and get bogged down in that day to day 'reality' of our lives. But being in your mind all the time is like being the only horse in a race that never ends. The mind tries to convince us that everything we see, hear and sense, is the truth. Our mind is the place where negative emotions rule the roost - anger, fear, worry, hate, judgement, disappointment, pain, sorrow, blame. It's the place where everything is about you, and you alone.

The mind tries to convince us that the person who we think we are inside our minds is who we really are. But that person is not who we really are, because in truth, we are all Universal.

Fortunately, we are always able to choose whether we think with our mind, or with our truth.

WHAT IS OUR TRUTH?

Our truth is our soul and is essentially love. It is a conscious, aware, happy, passionate, compassionate, forgiving and accepting us. Our truth has love and acceptance for everyone, without judgement

Love is the only real, consistent emotion that exists. Love is truth.

LOVE WITHOUT JUDGEMENT

Our truth, our soul, has no gender or race. The only thing that makes us male, female, intersex or otherwise is our sex and hormones. We are only these things here on Earth in the physical. Cultural background, colour, faith - these all give us a context for our experience.

When we deeply love or care for someone, a child for example, we love them from our truth, our soul. Not for one second when feeling that unconditional love does it cross our minds what colour we are, what our faith is, or whether we are male or female. It's just pure love, and love comes from the soul. It just *is*, and that is our truth and natural state. And that there is God, Universal.

The thing about the Universe/God is, there is no discrimination or judgement. Everyone, everything is equal, and a gift. Our differences are beautiful things that we can all learn from and experience with one another. We are all in this together, all connected to each other and presented to each other in the physical life for an experience. Without each other, there is no experience.

The differences between us make these experiences interesting, and give us novelty, something new. But too often we use our differences as an excuse to judge and be afraid of one another. If we watch little children playing with each other at a playground, we will see no judgement. Children that have never met each other before hold hands, hug, talk and laugh together. It's totally natural.

Why is that? Our soul is all we know when we are born. Our only memories are from inside the womb - there has been no human conditioning. A child has no idea about faith, gender or race. And the child doesn't care, because it doesn't matter. Children and babies are being who they naturally are, before the world they live in (their parents, society, environment) begin to condition them.

MIND CONDITIONING

Everyone becomes imprinted by our world. When we are born, we are all the same in our pure soul state. As we grow, our families, circumstances, societies that we are born into begin to tell us who we are. We are not born Catholic, Muslim, a Liberal, hippies – there are thousands of ways we classify and segregate ourselves. But we are none of these things until our minds are conditioned to think we are.

And that pure, natural state we were born in, can slowly get pushed back. But it is still there, because in actual fact, truth is all we really are. Truth is love, love is Universal. Does God judge? No, we humans do when we live in the mind. But if we remember who we really are, that we are Universal, we can overcome our mind conditioning and become in our physical life who we truly are.

Life, a thought

Judgement of the Mind

Not long ago the Earth was flat, slavery was still active in America, women couldn't vote or wear a bikini to the beach, the English ruled India, and there was something wrong with being gay. That's the mind. The mind is constant judgement. We can live our whole life a constant lie if we let our minds live us. Worse still, we can live others.

WHO ARE WE TRULY?

We all made a choice to be on this planet. Each one of us made a deal with the Universe (essentially with each other) before we came here to live on Earth to experience something specific – and that is our soul's journey.

In actual fact, we've all lived many life times. If we could remember all the lives we've ever had here on Earth, *this* life would be chaotic. We wouldn't be able to make decisions, take a risk, or evolve and grow. We would be too conditioned by everything we've experienced before. If we struggle with an experience that happened two days ago, what would it be like to remember 100 lifetimes of experiences? We wouldn't be able to handle it and process it all. We would be constantly living in the past, and the past is just that. Without movement, everything stops.

LEARNING FROM OUR MISTAKES

We all stuff up from time to time. We are human beings.

But mistakes are part of evolution, and always provide the opportunity for something new and different to happen, so a mistake is never really a mistake. Only us humans judge what the word "mistake" means. Without all my mistakes, I would have never ended up on that cliff, talking to the Universe and receiving this guide to happy. So, thank God for all those mistakes!

Now, I don't see one minute of my forty years before as anything but a great experience. Because, it all got me to where I am now. The difference between then and now is that I thought I was separate from the Universe and had no control over my life. I thought I had no control over my mind. See the words I just used then? I "thought" I had no control over my life and was separate! So, for 40 years, I was inventing with at least 60% of my mind.

Don't misunderstand, I've had some fantastic experiences in my life, but they were fleeting and didn't last. I can look back now and be forever grateful, but back then I didn't appreciate what I had. I was always worried I would lose it, and I was always chasing the next thing to try to find happiness. I can truthfully say, back then I had no fucking idea what it was I was even chasing.

If only I had just stopped for five minutes. Stopped for five minutes and got out of my mind, stopped thinking, I could have found my truth. It was always there! The keys were always in my hand. I was just looking everywhere else because it never occurred to me that happiness was actually already inside me. I wasn't conscious.

TRUTH AND MIND INVENTING

Free will allows us to choose with mind or truth. This is so we can invent our own life experience and what we want. We are not told what to do and never are, not by God. The Universe always delivers to us the experience we want to invent. You see, we are constantly inventing our experience. Whether we realise it or not, we are in control of our own destiny.

We have all heard inspiring stories of people escaping some terrible situations. The difference between the ones that do and the ones that don't, only ever comes down to how powerful their thought energy emotion is. The mind will tell us it's not possible, but our truth only knows it is. It's not the body that allows people to survive, it's the energy emotion behind their truthful thought.

We are all responsible for all our inventing and experiences. However, if you are or were anything like me before I received this understanding from the Universe, we are completely unaware of this. When we live in the mind, we too often find ourselves bitching and complaining about other people, what we don't have, how unhappy we are and so on and so on.

We call ourselves adults sometimes, but our minds can make us no different to a three-year-old child throwing a tantrum on the floor. The difference is a child can get out of their mind rather quickly because it is still innocent. A child isn't yet conditioned by human opinions, judgements, and right or wrongs of the mind. So, a child quickly goes back to being, and that's happy, truth and love. We are born as this.

As adults, if we are living in the mind we are much worse off than the child throwing the tantrum. When we are living in our minds, our whole life can become one big tantrum, a struggle with everything, day in day out.

Remember, we are our thoughts. We are inventing everything we put emotion to and bang on about. "I never wanted this," we say, "why does this keep happening to me"? Why the hell do we keep thinking and talking about it if we don't want it to happen? We must think about what we *do* want. It really is just a choice of whether we use our mind or our truth.

When we become conscious of our truth, we can catch ourselves when we are in our minds. The mind is always there trying to pull us back in, and it often does, but with awareness we notice this happening, and can stop it. It's like getting fit. The fitter you are, the easier it is.

IT'S ALL FOR YOU

Believe this and be open to this - and you clearly are: you wouldn't have read this far if you weren't open or finding your truth. That's fact. You just made that sentence happen. Keep reading, it makes sense.

Every single person you meet that comes into and out of your life, someone you see crossing the road in front of you, someone you think may be being nasty to you, someone that is very caring and loving to you, someone you see on your way to work you may never see again, a homeless person in the street…

ALL of it is for you! All of it. It has been invented for you to experience. Without any of what happens around you, there is nothing to gauge anything from, or anything to invent the experience that your thought energy is creating.

All of it is for you. We need to be aware of how fortunate we all are. We all now know what thought energy emotion does, so we must accept that it's always been us doing our own inventing. Has it been with mind or truth? Only you know the answer to that.

Man, the relief I had when the Universe explained this to me was massive. To know it was me! I was in total control of inventing my life?! Fuck did I laugh at myself. I was on cloud nine all of a sudden.

I didn't dive back into my past and start beating myself up, because I realised that wasn't going to help. But I was able to truthfully say the Universe had absolutely given me everything I wanted, I was just inventing with my mind and getting what I focused my thoughts on.

WE ARE THE INVENTORS, BUT CAN'T PUSH AGAINST OUR SOUL'S PURPOSE

Many things we experience in life, we may think we didn't want, but how do we know what we wanted to physically experience before we were born? We don't! We don't need to know everything. We will never know everything and if we did, it would be boring, and the end of evolution.

But, if we live our truth the best we can, we will live an awesome life. Just *being*, not swimming against the riptide, and being conscious. When it's with truth, we are it. Free will lets us choose. How good is that? We don't know what truth is without the mind, but truth is what makes us remember who we really are.

THANK YOU FOR…

So, maybe a thank you is a better way forward. Your world is being invented for you. All the other souls are here to help invent your experience for you. Yes, it's absolute.

The people, or souls, here on Earth have all played a part in inventing all my experiences. Everything in my life I have invented, and all of you have played a part and helped me with that. Without you all, I had or have nothing. My thought energy – whether with my mind or truth at the time - invented my experience. Then whatever my vibration was, the people I needed to come into my life for my experience, did. And a lot of those people I treated badly.

I personally and sincerely with love, would like to apologise to anyone I've ever hurt, or told to fuck off in my past. I am sincerely sorry. I was in my mind at the time and had no clue of what you were doing for me. I was making my own movie and you were part of the cast that I asked for, so I thank you with all I have.

Remember, we are part of everyone else's life inventing also. So, if we are conscious of what's going on, why not send a bit of love out there? Maybe a thank you to the Universe for every single circumstance that crosses our path. This is the way forward. Watch your world change. We are free. Stop, breathe, take a minute. Feel the wind, the sun, or nothing at all. Notice the Universe, and it will notice you back.

Life, a thought

No Different

A bee helps pollinate a flower, in return, the bee receives pollen from the flower for honey. Without each other, they don't evolve. Humans are no different. We are all here for each other. Without each other, we don't evolve. When we become grateful for each other, watch our world change.

CHAPTER 4

KNOWING MIND OR TRUTH

HOW DOES TRUTH INVENTING WORK?

This is the fun part. Every thought we have creates something. It can be miniscule and barely noticed, even missed, or it can be mega big. It depends on the emotion we give to it. We know that thought invents a vibration as everything is energy. Our held onto thought energy is then manifested into the physical.

When we remember and know our truth, there are infinite options available to us. Infinite opportunities for excitement for life, people, love, gratitude, happiness and laughter. Our life never ever ends!

KNOWING TRUTH

Sometimes the mind will have us thinking negative thoughts of ourselves. It will also tell us other people think negative thoughts of us and we are not of value. Stop right there! The Universe delivers to us whatever our mind or our truth is holding on to, so letting the mind carry us away with negative thoughts will only bring more of the same.

Remember, truth is love, happiness, laughter, being who we naturally are, and love for yourself. This is consciousness, this is who we are. Reach for your truth. You've got it, right there. You *are* it.

Once your thought energy emotion is truth, you are inventing awesome experiences, no matter what, and awesome people will be coming into your life. That's what you'll be inventing. Great shit happens with truth.

THE MIND = SWIMMING AGAINST THE RIPTIDE

A little while back, I would catch a ferry each morning to work in Sydney, Australia. My work wasn't my passion, and I didn't like what I was doing. I was chasing a dream I thought I needed to make my life "happy". Every time I got on that ferry I felt like a lead weight, dragging the ferry down. It was like we were pushing through concrete, not water. And my vibration was slowing everyone else down on that ferry too.

But after the Universe answered my questions and gave me this guide, it was clear as day what I was doing wrong. I was chasing a dream that didn't belong to me or my truth. It was a perception that my mind had made up and it wasn't what I wanted. I was living out a conditioned life, doing what I had been told and thought I needed to do to be happy.

My soul's radar had been constantly trying to tell me I was off track. It does all the time, we just need to listen. We think that all that exists is what we see. The mind does this. Remember, what we can't see makes up a trillion times more than what we can. When something doesn't feel good, we are pushing against our truth and we a swimming against the riptide. Nothing about my job felt right, but I was ignoring that feeling because I was so conditioned to think I was doing all the right things that would lead to happiness.

OUR INBUILT RADAR TO TRUTH, THE ANSWER IS ALWAYS THERE

We are all Universal and connected to the one consciousness. We are 1000 times more powerful than any battleships radar out at sea, or any satellite orbiting the Earth. Our in-built radar to truth will help us find the answer to any important decision. All we must do is ask, "Will this, and does this feel happy"?

Stop and feel the answer inside. Give it some space to feel it. Our whole life is about understanding with what emotion we are using. When we realise that, the rest comes easy. If it truthfully feels right, it is. If it feels good, there is your answer.

Truth emotion is our soul telling us we are swimming with the riptide. This is the Universe answering us. It is always in us and the Universe ALWAYS answers. You are connected, and the Universe isn't somewhere else. More on how to actually do this later on.

Truth and Mind

Truth: Swimming with the riptide. There are different paths we take, a move to the left or right. This is our inventing and experiencing here on Earth. Our souls purpose. It always takes us where we are going. Living with our truth equals happiness. It's all exciting when we are conscious of the game we are in. Its life.

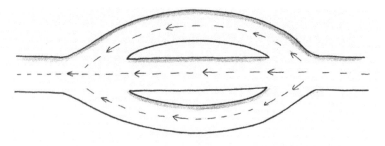

Mind: Anger, fear, worry, self-doubt, judgement, separate, opinions, negativity. The mind is like a Los Angeles freeway. Its swimming against a riptide. When we get caught in this, it's a mess. Little to say about the mind except, there is no happiness there.

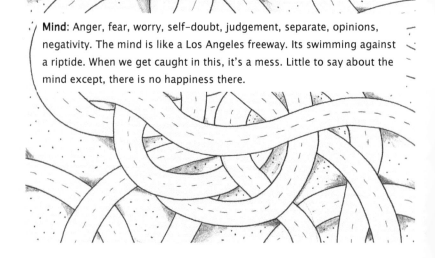

WE CAN'T CONTROL OTHERS

We cannot control anyone or anyone else's life or thoughts - ever. We never want to when we live with our truth because we accept everyone as they are. They are living in their world, having their experience. Our truth and who we are always comes out anyway, so a person that tries to control another never, ever wins.

Control over any other person is not done with truth. Your mind is essentially trying to beat God. Good luck with that one.

LETTING OTHERS LIVE THEIR TRUTH

We can share our truth with someone, because it comes from a place of love, but we don't want to force our truth on anyone else. As much as we may love them and want them to experience what we think will be the best thing for them. It may not be their soul's journey, or their truth. Often, we are mistaken on ownership. Many parents for example, think they own their children. The only thing we have ownership over is our thoughts.

My 13-year-old son recently told me his mother really wants him to go to university. Now, my son is a bit of a free spirit, loves surfing and being outside with nature. That's his gig and his truth.

He told me he would like to be a tradesman and work outside, rather than have an inside job. Just the thought of being inside and having to attend more schooling than he has to, has him feeling like he's swimming against the biggest riptide he could imagine. But, he also doesn't want to disappoint his mum, and knows she just wants what's best for him.

His thought energy inventing already has him thinking

about how much he hates the idea of college. If he keeps this up, by the time he gets to 17, no good will come of it.

LIVE YOUR TRUTH, NOT OTHERS

Trying to do something else against our truth to make someone else happy has us pushing shit uphill. What we think would make someone else happy is often just what would make us happy for them, and not necessarily the thing that would make *them* happy. That's why we cannot force our truth on others. We can recommend, and make suggestions, but our life movie is not theirs. We are just part of their cast as they are ours.

Everyone else is the main actor and the director of their own movie. When we don't live our truth and swim against the riptide, it ends in unhappiness. We already know it when we are doing it. If it feels that hard, is that hard, and there is no passionate thought emotion behind it, we are not living our truth. We are living someone else's.

My son's mother only wants what is best for him, and she believes this is a university education. This belief comes from a place of love, but it's also partly her fear of him not having, which she thinks will make him happy. But that there is her truth, her movie, not his.

OUR PURPOSE

Our soul has a purpose here on Earth as we have discussed, and not many of us know what that is. In fact, my son could have been a workaholic in his previous life. He could have just walked past his friends, family and children and never given them the time of day. He could have missed all the beauty that nature has to offer and just spent his whole life in an office, living in the mind and missed so much and with much regret. We can't know that was the case, but it's possible.

Who's to say his purpose in this life isn't to experience all that he missed in his previous life and further evolve? His soul has a purpose, and if he pushes against that his whole life will be a struggle.

If we live our truth with love and allow others to live theirs as they will, and expect nothing from others, all they get is love. What comes from that? Awesomeness! It's so much easier, and it feels great.

HEART ENERGY

This energy comes from what is called the heart chakra located behind the heart. Nothing to do with the physical heart. An open heart is giving. The more of this we give away the more we receive, and it keeps building, it gets bigger. Unlike a car that runs out of petrol, the Universe sees this and tops up your tank, and your tank just gets bigger and bigger. This is done with our Truth and love. Its what makes "you", feel good. You get it back.

CHAPTER 5

WHAT LIVING NOW MEANS

YESTERDAY CAN BECOME TODAY, AND TOMORROW CAN BECOME YESTERDAY. EVERY DAY CAN BECOME YESTERDAY IF WE LET IT.

Our past, present and future is right now. Here! It's *all* here now, at this second.

We can actually live our whole life in the past, today. Many of us may have had what we call traumatic experiences in our past. Every time we think back to that experience, we are reliving that experience, right now, like it is happening today. Doing this can give that unpleasant experience from our past more life, increasing its effect on us and allowing it to have a greater emotional impact. Remembering and going back over the experience actually increases its presence and power, and we experience more of the same. I did this for many years. All it did was fuck me up more and more, and it was on repeat.

Remember, what we hold on to, we invent. Once we accept the past and acknowledge that it happened, we can wave it goodbye immediately. Or, we cannot accept it, and we can remain there, even now.

Remembering is a fantastic thing and can stop us experiencing more pain, but using our thought energy to invent great experiences now and in the future is what we want to be conscious of. You see, we can live our past and the future NOW, this very second. We now know that the thought energy we put to anything invents our lives, and that it's up to us to choose what we put our thought energy to. We need to be conscious of whether we are inventing with our minds or truth.

Let's try something. Let's remember a loving, happy, positive experience from our past, right now. Put yourself there and re-live what happened. Can you feel the thought emotion from that memory being brought back to life? It's always there whenever we need to draw on it for inspiration, to help us invent now, in this second, and in the future.

Life, a thought

Surfing a change

If the same wave was to reform every time exactly the same, it would become boring. Same goes for listing to just one song repeatedly for ever.

Without change, there is no experience. Change is the only thing that makes anything great, great.

YOU ARE NOT YOUR PAST

Living in the now has been talked about often, but I never had any clue what it really meant till the Universe explained it to me in my terms. It's super important to be conscious of *now*, as you read this.

Think back to your past - three, six months, even a year, two or five. Can you think of something you did that makes you say, "I can't believe I did that! What the fuck was I thinking?!" Personally, I can think of hundreds!

Why? Because that person is not who we are anymore, it's not who we are *now*. Whatever the situation was, it was something that we invented with our thought emotion, and again it was our thought emotion that got us to here at this point, but it's still not who we are now. Our thoughts and emotions in the present now are constantly inventing our future, our present and past. Every minute of every day.

Your past is not who you are now. Your past is a total sum of who you were, the culmination of your thought emotion and experience that has got you to this exact point. And it is at this point, right now, that the future starts. Here, in this moment. We can start fresh as fuck and change our future right now if we want to.

FIRST, FORGIVENESS

So, the first thing we must do here now is forgive ourselves of anything we may regret and forgive others. This doesn't mean we are condoning anything, it just means we can move on. It's done and doesn't belong to us anymore. We have essentially reincarnated ourselves right here, NOW. Not anyone else. Us. You! We are free. Release anything we no longer want or want our minds to keep pulling us back into. Only our mind judges us and others.

NOW FIRE UP

Forgive, say goodbye, and we are starting fresh NOW.

When the Universe told me this I bawled my eyes out. So much weight and bullshit I'd been carrying for years had been lifted. It will continue to lift over time, but now we are following the *Universal Guide to Happy*.

Every minute of every day has provided an experience that our soul has grown from. Everything gets us to a point. There is no such thing as an accident – our thought energy inventing has created all of our experiences. Things may have happened in the past that we consider negative, shitty experiences. But in fact, they can be a blessing. It might not seem like it, but they have contributed to getting us to this point, where we are understanding our ability to invent the future we want, using our thought energy.

What ever thought and emotion we are putting to anything now, we are inventing.

So, check this out: where we are now, sitting here reading this has already happened. We are living in the past right now.

WTF? HOW? WHY?

Our past thoughts, three, six, twelve months ago – whatever - imagined this with mind or truth emotion, and invented it. "Yes!", some of us will say, "this is just what I've been after!"

But if you just read that sentence and said to yourself, "the fuck I wanted this!" you may not have *consciously* wanted it, but your thought energy emotion was focused on it, so here we are. It can't be denied. It's Universal. You invent, and that's what you experience.

And so, we have caught up to our past. Truthfully, go back to three, six, twelve months, and ask yourself your truth. Are we where we are now because of our thoughts and emotions back then? Back then was once now. Back then invented now. Trust the Universe, it was.

NOW, WE ARE NATURE IN MOTION

Here is how now thoughts invent our future. But where we are "now", was invented back then. Imagine a deciduous tree going through its seasons. When a tree loses all its leaves and looks dead, that's actually when it's at its most alive. We can't see this, as it looks completely dormant to the eye. But all the trees cells are buzzing with energy, creating the buds that will sprout into the leaves and flowers that we will see in six to twelve weeks' time. What we see when a tree is in full bloom was actually created weeks and months ago. When it looks its most alive, it's actually finished its cycle. Resting and enjoying - you could even call it dying. Well part of it is, it's reincarnating.

Reincarnating. We do it every night when we go to sleep, but are not conscious of it. Part of us dies every night and we wake up changed, different every single day. Our bodies are older, even opinions of rights and wrongs, or what we may have thought about a particular subject yesterday.

So, we as humans are no different to trees in nature. The only difference is the tree knows exactly what it's doing, and we as humans mostly have no idea. The tree lives every moment now, and creates every future moment, now. The tree just is and goes with the flow of what it is.

Everything and every future experience is created now. Our thoughts right now are the key to our future and what we want to experience.

Wrap our heads around it! We have caught up to ourselves. The future you is already happening/happened. Yep, it is... but we can change it right now if we want to. If we are happy, don't change a thing. But what we must realise is that this is all happening now, and is always happening now.

We now understand the power of thought energy emotion, truth and mind, and they invent all our past, present and future experiences. Giddy up!

NOW VIBRATION - PRESENT, PAST AND FUTURE

It's amazing what pain can invent. Without pain there seems to be a lack of wanting, or drive for better. Physical pain and non-physical pain can be such a laugh when we think about it. Why? Because honestly, *life* is such a laugh when we take ourselves out of our minds. We've all stubbed our toe at some time or another, or even hit our elbow. It hurts like hell, but we often find ourselves laughing. We are laughing at the same time we say, "Fuck me this hurts"!

Many of our past experiences are exactly this when we look back at them with Universal perspective. The peaks and troughs make up our life experience.

When we are conscious, the pain is not felt as much. Pain is our thought about something that is happening at any point in time. Pain brings about change: it's what we do with it that counts. Used the right way it's incredibly powerful and positive. This can be incredibly hard to see at times, especially when we are living in our mind, perhaps in the thick of a difficult situation or event, such as the death of a loved one. But eventually, the Universe will prove it to be true.

INVENTING WHAT WE WANT NOW, INVENTS OUR EXPERIENCE NOW, MORE OF THE PAST, AND OUR FUTURE

A friend of mine recently broke up with his girlfriend. She left him for another man and he was absolutely shattered. His mind and ego was hurt. He's a good-looking man, confident, very charming, and the ladies really love him… usually. But for about six months he couldn't for the life of him get a woman to notice him. All he wanted was to find was another girlfriend to make him feel happiness and fill his empty space. The more he tried, the further away it got.

He ended up speaking to me about it. 'Jake,' he said, "It's like they can smell failure on me!' Geeze, his comment made me laugh. The thought energy vibration he was inventing for himself with his mind was so obvious, and I knew I could help him.

'They can't smell anything,' I replied. 'It's your thought energy vibration of yourself that they can't feel. It's not matching theirs – they literally can't see you. Like the wind, you are there, but totally invisible to the eye. You're walking around thinking negative thoughts about yourself, being worried about not being noticed, not picking up, so how could you attract a positive woman? They can sense that negative vibration. Remember, we are all vibrating energy. If your vibration is low, and the girls you are attracted to are high and positive, your vibrations won't match."

We talked about how the thoughts we have invent everything, and how his thoughts of himself over the last three months since his girlfriend left him, as he put it, were all negative. These thoughts left him thinking he wasn't worthy.

'Your past thoughts invented this experience,' I explained. 'You have allowed yourself, your mind, your ego, to be conditioned by an experience that happened months ago. Then you held onto it, fed it with emotion, and now you're living it. You've invented this experience.'

He looked pretty glum about this, to be honest, but I hadn't got to the part where he realised he could change it all by thinking with his truth, and creating positive thought emotion to invent what he really wanted.

'Listen mate,' I said. 'Did your girlfriend leave you, or did she do you a favour? Remember, we are all watching and inventing different movies. How do you know her leaving even had anything to do with you? Your mind/ego is living you, not your truth.'

He was soon able to see how his thought energy and emotion was inventing what he didn't want and how easily he could change his future. Within two weeks he was back in his driver's seat, with positive thought energy inventing a better experience for himself. It was only ever his negative thoughts of himself that were stopping him doing this. Our minds spin bullshit stories that are not our truth, all the time.

CHANGING NOW, NOW

Negative thoughts of self and others absolutely invents that life experience. When we become conscious of that, we drop negative thought like the plague. Always think highly of yourself and others. It's a sure way to make us feel great, and it invents more of the same!

It's that simple and can be that fast. Don't think of the past if it's not what you want anymore. Imagine the future. Imagine it the best you can. Make it as happy as you can. Pick just one positive thing that puts an instant smile on your face. Just one thing and hold on to it. If you can pick three or five, do it and hold on to each thought for one minute each. Do it as often as you can.

Hold on to it and don't lose the emotion. Believe it. Know it to be true. Write down what you just imagined so you won't forget. You are now inventing your future life experiences. Yes, it has started right now, this second!

Remember there is space between every thought, and it becoming your reality. The space is there to make sure you really do want it. Be aware and hold on to it, hold on to it, hold on to it! If you can picture yourself as anything, you can be it. There are no limits except that of the mind. That is Universal.

Life, a thought

Conditioning

Does the sun rise? Does the sun set?

We have been taught that the sun rises and the sun sets. It's perspective.

It's what our eyes and mind want to see and believe.

The sun never rises and never sets. Earth orbits the sun, rotates.

Earth meets the sun in the morning and leaves it behind in the afternoon.

CHAPTER 6

UNDERSTANDING OPINIONS
AND CONDITIONING

WHAT ARE OPINIONS?

That sounds like a pretty basic question, and I never really gave it much thought. One answer could be an opinion is someone's thoughts on a particular subject, which is true. Opinions come down to mind or truth. Being conscious or not. It's quite easy to give an opinion on any given subject without having all the facts.

Here's the catch: even if we did have all the facts, which is impossible, these facts are often made up of opinions given by many other people. So, we can pass on someone else's opinion as our own, without even realising it.

One thing the universe was very clear to me about was, be conscious about giving an opinion that criticises someone personally, or to try to cut them down. Our thought vibration becomes negative, and we then draw that into our lives. The reaction can be instant, and not what we wanted either.

Plus, we have done nothing to help the other person. They are part of our cast and we have just given them a terrible experience. Emotionally, we have both lost. No one has benefited here. The other option is giving truth with love and trying help them. Personally, I take the latter now. The amount of times I got punched in the mouth from my words…. I can't even count.

When someone picks us up off the ground we feel great, cared for. When we pick someone else up off the ground, *we* feel great. It feels right. That's our truth. We are all in this together, separate to nothing.

A friend of mine (let's call her Sal) was recently going through a challenging few months and was seeking opinions from her friends on her current life issues. Sal told me about a few negative experiences she was having with her friends' opinions that hurt her emotionally. Sal was living in her mind at the time and was taking on other people's opinions about her life experiences as gospel. She believed them and started living them deeply.

Sal hated her job, her apartment, not having a partner, and many other things. Her friends were rather quick to point out how much they would hate to live her life. Her thought vibration was attracting these friends. She was so in her mind. She would even get offended if someone said they didn't like her hand bag.

If we focus on what's wrong, we invent more of what's wrong. If we believe a negative opinion, what are we inventing for ourselves? And is it even true, does it belong to you? When we are not grateful for anything, we only see what we don't have. No good comes from it.

With the Universal guide I was able to help her with truth opinion. We focused on what's right, changed the thought and imagination emotion. My opinion even made me feel great. We started to focus on what she was really good at and loved doing. We even started to laugh about what Sal thought were negative experiences and found the funny side in them. Suddenly, they became obsolete. We were onto positive inventing mode.

Then we both started to imagine and fantasise about *what if*? We thought about and painted a fantastic, positive picture about who she wanted to be and what she wanted to invent for herself. We were inventing it right there, right then. She was laughing! She was there already, but still here. But right here now, her thought energy emotion was inventing her future, but she was also living that emotion right now. Now she was aware of her inventing, and what opinions really matter or not.

That's what a truth opinion for others can invent. It's a collective effort and we invent happy for all of us. That's Universal.

BEING AWARE OF MIND OPINIONS

When we have two or more people judging and thinking with their mind emotion, we have a guaranteed stuff up in the making. Who knows how many other opinions have been dragged into the whole thing along the way? This is how the mind spreads bullshit that doesn't belong to us. We can end up believing it and being it. We become part of it.

Not so long ago, back in the 1900s and even early 2000s, a lot of people thought there was something wrong with being gay. Hell, it was a crime – against the law. Whose mind was this, and whose opinion was it that made this law? What right did they have to judge anyone on right or wrong? Who gets to say what is right or wrong anyway? God doesn't judge, but we humans do. Today, it's practically impossible to believe this history. We can't fathom such a backward thought now!

Consider the lion heart a gay person had to have to tell their truth twenty years ago. Wow. To live their truth, they had to front up against all the conditioned minds and judgements of their society. This goes for all of those that made a stand for equality across the board.

What was previously considered wrong, we can't even imagine being so now. It was the result of conditioning and opinions of the mind on a grand scale, passed down from generation to generation, until our collective truth could no longer bear it, and change finally happened.

Opinions given without truth or love for others are like terminal cancer.

We've all been judgmental in the past and to say we haven't, well, that would probably be bullshit. Everyone, everyone has some kind of secret they are not particularly proud of or are self-conscious of. How is any one judgment any different from another? Is there a sliding scale of right and wrong? What one person finds right or wrong, differs to the next. What might deeply offend one person, another might not even give two shits about. Whose judgement or opinion is wrong or right, then? There isn't one! It's an opinion.

The opinions we hold can become us. Thought + emotion + spoken word = what we invent, and the Universe is always making this happen for us. We may think voicing our opinion is just the passing on of an idea, or harmless information, but we are separate from nothing, particularly our spoken word.

We too need to stay conscious of what we invent with every day - truth or mind.

Life, a thought

Does your opinion belong to you?

How many people worry about not owning a property or investment property these days? In the Western world anyway. Why, whose truth or thought is that? Does it even belong to you? Or has it been passed down over time through our parents, societies and financial institutions.

How many monks' living in the Himalayas are worried about how many properties they own? I wonder what their truth is. Just a little something to think about. It doesn't make either one right or wrong, but it is only our truth that matters.

THE TRAP OF DRAMA AND CONDITIONING

Some of us absolutely love drama. But this just gives the mind a sense of purpose. The ones of us that love drama and create a shit fight are the ones that are most unhappy. I lived this. Our minds feed off drama because it justifies why we feel so terrible or unhappy. If others feel terrible and unhappy also, it must be right, right? And there it is. Anything that feels bad is our mind pushing against our truth (soul). Our thought vibration is off track. Our soul is telling us this. It's the slap in the face. "Snap out of it", it's saying.

The mind can be conditioned from a very early age. As children, if we are brought up being told we are hopeless, we are worthless, we are not loved, or even given a reason to think these types of things, this has an imprint. Like a branding on cattle, only in our minds. As children we watch and listen to our parent's and other adults' behaviour around us. We can then live out our adult life entirely based on this past conditioning.

Once we become conscious we no longer judge. Awareness helps us understand we really don't know others life movies. You see, some parents are labelled "shitty parents", but we really have no idea of their upbringing and will never know. When we except this (we must to move on) we can wave goodbye to any childhood experience we no longer want or want to dwell on. The second we do we are free. We can start living our souls' purpose and stop trying to live others.

CONDITIONED OPINIONS
PASSED ON, OR BROKEN

I'm going to use a friend's childhood story here, let's call them "Simon." Simon's childhood is a great example of conditioning that gave him understanding. There is no longer any pain associated to it and Simon rarely gives it any thought, apart from the fact it was a blessing that broke generations of conditioning.

Here is what Simon told me. From about the age of four to eleven, there was no love in Simon's house hold. In its place there was violence. In his home life, he was constantly told how hopeless he was and smacked around a lot. This came out in his behaviour in the school playground.

This became his thought of himself, who he believed he was. Simon thought it was normal to be smacked around and to be told he was useless and believed it. How he felt about himself is how he treated others. "I remember wanting to go to school so I wasn't at home, and when it was nearing the end of a school day, wishing it wouldn't end so I wouldn't have to go home. I was constantly in the principal's office getting the cane. Again, getting more of what I got at home, but it was better than home, so again I thought it was normal."

I personally know Simon very well and have a good idea where he is coming from. Simon had been conditioned by other people's anger and negative opinions of themselves and that had been passed onto him. He believed it. He has since forgiven them. It did not belong to him. He was a product of something in front of them that they could express their lack of love and own self-hatred to. It could have been anyone in front of them, but Simon was that anyone. Their minds were hell. They were living hell here on Earth. There is no condoning this behaviour, but we can at least understand where it comes from. When we think someone is being nasty to us, or being a bully, (troll) we need stop for a minute and look at them. What they are doing to you, and how they are trying to make you feel, is *exactly* what they think of themselves. They actually don't realise it, of course. There is a major lack of self-love and confidence inside. Remember, what we can't see is so much greater than what we can.

How they feel about themselves does not belong to us. A bully (troll) can make others' life hell, but only if we allow their opinion or actions to become part of us. We need to change our thought energy vibration to what we want to invent, and pass that on. This is hard to do as children as we are not conscious of the power of thought energy.

The Universe made me clear on this. We can turn an adverse childhood upbringing in to something positive. It's a choice. When we are conscious, the choice would be not to repeat it. We can show our children they are loved, no matter what. To live their TRUTH with love for themselves and with love for everything and everyone around them. We also have compassion for others who may have been "branded" and are now living in the mind. Simon lives by this. So, turns out Simon's childhood was a blessing.

When we live with our truth, we are free and don't care because we don't judge others. We are all human, we get angry and frustrated from time to time, but when we are living consciously we acknowledge that everyone is living their own life movie, and the only thing we can control is our thought energy. So, an opinion that doesn't create a whole pile of shit for someone else, or others close to them, is far more beneficial to all of us. And it feels right. It feels great!

OPINIONS ARE CONSTANTLY FAULTED

Let's think about science. Science is what we as human beings believe and accept as validation of fact, or as evidence of why things are the way they are. Wow, is that right? Science *constantly* proves itself wrong. The Earth was once flat, remember? Opium was used for headaches, and to settle babies to sleep. The concept of humans creating a machine that could fly was considered lunacy. All opinions.

Don't get me wrong. Science is fantastic and is constantly making mind-blowing discoveries that help civilisation, otherwise known as evolution, and we use it as a way to give validation to a point we are trying to make. But it is still an opinion in the end, and one that is constantly changing, as is everything else, and always will.

The only one thing we can ever rely on is we are all one, and that is the only one thing that will always remain the same. Remember what Universal means? Love is the only thing that is real and constant. Every single person on this planet who has ever experienced true love of any kind will give you the same opinion on love: it feels friggin' great! It always does, and is the only one consistent thing that never, ever changes.

LIFE MOVIE OPINIONS

When we think we know someone or their world (their life movie) we really have no idea. None.

When our partner, child, mother, father, friend or whomever leaves our sight, they are living in a whole different world to ours. The people they meet, other friends they interact with, we have absolutely no idea about. We couldn't even imagine what their life movie looks like. We will never actually know their inventing. All we get is a glimpse of what they allow us to see while we are interacting with them now.

That there is what we must accept. When someone is frustrated, angry, or disgruntled about something or another, we are going to get an opinion of someone that is frustrated, angry or perhaps in the mind. Who knows what their experience has brought them today. When we look for opinions of other people, it is best to look within someone that feels happy to us, or whose vibration feels right. Someone we respect. We will know this is the right person as soon as they open their mouth to give us their opinion, sometimes even before.

Have you ever asked a positive person you respect what they think about a particular person, even someone that is generally thought of as despicable or arrogant? They will either say, "I don't really know them" (which is, of course, 100% true), or "I don't have an opinion". Or, they will find a positive trait in that person or subject. When we are conscious and non-judgemental, we stay away from negative inventing at all costs.

On another hand, we will always find someone else who has an opinion on everything, even things they know nothing at all about. These people can throw negative opinions about like confetti! I knew this person well. This person was me!

This is normally someone caught right up in their mind. This is a person that needs a bit of self-love, and sometimes all that takes is a little understanding and a bit of love from someone else. Why not throw them some love? It's free, and the Universe sees it. Thought energy vibration remember... it's coming back to you. We are all in this together. Give it away and it will come back to you.

GOOD NEWS, TRUTH OPINION

The good news is it looks like there is a big swing back to consciousness and many of us are getting back to who we really are. Our truth. These changes and rules of past minds are revealing our truth to us, who we really are. It cannot be hidden. It's too powerful. Truth is LOVE, the only real emotion that is consistent. Happiness doesn't lay in stuff, happiness is inside of us, once we remember.

The main thing we must always remember is that love is the only real emotion we have that is consistent. It's the only real thing that is true and *always* feels great. There's also a saying, "don't believe everything you see or hear". Whenever you think something is a good idea, just sit on it for a minute first to make sure it's not your mind/ego at play.

Both are very valid, and I consciously do my best to live by these two things. They help with eliminating judgement.

Also remember that who we are now is not who we were in the past. It has been part of our life inventing. Whether it was from prior conditioning, opinions, or mind it doesn't matter one bit. We are accepting it (have accepted it) and we are moving on to understanding. When we understand and accept, the rest flows. We are swimming with the riptide and it's *so* easy to move on. We just veer off to the side, a gentle move to the left or right to change our course and invent what we want.

Our whole life is like this. It's a simple as stepping from one side of a line to the other. Truth be known, we do it all the time, we just aren't conscious of it. It's a game, remember. We wanted it. Trust ourselves, we wanted this life.

We are separate from nothing. Give away the good and you will get it. When we accept others, we can do this with compassion and love. We are never offended when we are aware of mind or truth opinion.

Truth, love opinion, not for us, but ALL of us. It's free and it equals happy. It does. The rest doesn't need thought.

Life, a thought

Right Wrong

When we think we are so right, proven a point and won, we have lost.

The only winner here is the Ego/Mind.

Consciousness and intelligence comes in accepting we are both.

CHAPTER 7

I AM

I AM WHAT I PUT I AM TO

Recently, I was walking through a mall with a friend of mine in Sydney, Australia. There were lots of people busking, singing, playing guitar, and all that good stuff. There was a young kid, about fifteen smashing away at a drum kit. Boy, could this kid play! In front of his kit he had written a sign, "All donations go to cystic fibrosis".

I was curious. I waited till the kid had finished his piece and asked, "Do all donations really go to cystic fibrosis?"

"Yep," he replied, "I am cystic fibrosis! All donations go to me!"

My god, did I laugh! It was his truth and his I Am.

What a positive kid. With positive thought he was able to turn cystic fibrosis on its head and really make it work for him. It was his truth, his thought, and boy was he going with the riptide. Often, we feel sorry for people with disabilities or what we may think is a disability. I know first-hand this isn't the case. We may not all be conscious of why things are happening at the time, but eventually I was able to realise that what we label the bad and difficult things in our lives are a gift.

I AM THE DOWNS, THE TROUGHS, THE PAIN AND THE PEAKS

Let's throw an example out there – Stephen Hawking. His motor neuron disease was a gift, and a gift for so many of us. The disease looked like a difficult life from a physical point of view, (our movie) but it brought out his best. Look at the discoveries he made. Would he have made all those discoveries if he was physically mobile? Who's to say.

You see, what we think, or imagine, about something can be so opposite to what *is*, when it comes to someone else's point of view, their life and inventing. How can a disease or disability be a good thing? It's what we do with it that makes it a blessing or not. Consciousness is a blessing, no matter what form it comes in.

So, a thought of sorrow, or feeling sorry for someone, doesn't help them one bit. Thought energy vibration, remember - we feel it. We are better off throwing them a thought of "Good on you! More power to you!". That's a great vibration to send someone. We don't know their life movie or what they are inventing. We don't have any clue to what their souls' purpose is here on Earth.

How about this for a thought? Someone in a wheelchair for example, may be flying! We may be the ones walking around, thinking we are the fortunate ones and feeling sorry for them. But we actually have no idea of the potential consciousness/ experience that being in a wheelchair might be giving them. They may not even be aware of it themselves. In fact, the able-bodied people may be the unfortunate ones, and the people with disabilities are the ones that are flying and consciously evolving.

It's what we do with what we've got. When we are in something, anything, it's about how we use our thought energy vibration to make it work for us.

CHAPTER 8

I AM INVENTING

I AM MY BODY... OR AM I?

We are very attached to our bodies, nearly consumed how our shell looks or doesn't look.

Conditioning has played a part in this. But our bodies are on loan from the Universe. It's great to be proud and healthy to enjoy a quality of life, but our bodies are not who we are. They really aren't! It's what's inside the shell that matters and makes us, *us*. When we become consumed by how our shell looks, we are no different to a kid dressing up a doll or putting a goat in a suit. It's a life lived in the mind, on the surface.

The outside is an illusion of what the mind thinks is real. We need physicality to exist here on Earth, but being consumed by our outside appearance too often brings unhappiness. And in actual fact, keeps us concerned about what other people's opinions are of us. Remember, trying to guess what other people think of us or not is absolutely insane! It does not help one bit and is not our truth. It's the mind playing with us.

What I am, I am, and I am forever grateful. It's my movie and my experience and I would never want to take any of it back.

I AM INVENTING

The words "I am", held onto for long enough, with strong emotion, is what we become. We are what we think we are, but we are also what we think we are not. It's Universal. If we are thinking, imagining it, it's a thought and we are inventing it or bringing it closer toward us, depending on the emotion behind it.

Fear and lack of often brings to us exactly that. We are inventing with our thought energy vibration. We can imagine being millionaires, but only if we focus 80% of our emotion on how much we're going to enjoy being financially secure, or what holiday we may go on. Not on how broke we are. We can imagine meeting our awesome partner, but must imagine with our emotion how exciting it is to fall in love, and to care deeply and intimately for someone. It's not going to happen if we fixate on how lonely we are, or keep wondering where they are. That then is what we keep inventing, our virtual reality hologram.

Remember, emotion = feeling, passion about anything.

Motion = absolute movement of anything. Visible or not, such as wind, thought and sound.

The best way to get what we want is write down with passion what we want or want to be with I AM. If we keep doing that and hold onto it with emotion, we invent it. Just like in the illustration of 4D life hologram.

Writing things down keeps us focused on what we want and helps to bridge that space between our thought and experiencing what we want in reality. Write each thing down three times to really drum it in. Once we've written down everything we want to invent and experience that is important to us, we then read it aloud. We must also focus on what that is, or what it looks like, smells like and feels like with emotion.

Remember, find the thing or things that put a smile on your face. What are you passionate about? Thought energy in a state of happy and love emotion is incredibly powerful in inventing your experience and bringing it into physical life. Remember, if you really want to make your thought energy powerful, speak it. The thought invents the sound. A spoken word creates a sound, a sound is vibrating energy and so is the Universe and all of us.

Life, a thought

Be it

We all have thoughts and imagine and fantasise about who we want to be. Often, we wave them off like they are not possible, like it is separate to us.

But, if you just thought it and imagined it, you are it already! Yes.

Remember there is space between thought energy. Hold onto it because you are it if you want to be.

This is what people do that inspire us. The only difference is they imagined it, thought it, held onto it with powerful emotion, and became it.

They were already living it before it happened.

EXAMPLE: I AM CONSCIOUSLY
INVENTING MY LIFE NOW

I am finding a great partner.
I am finding a great partner.
I am finding a great partner.

Imagine what that looks like, feels like, smells like, and you are already inventing that now. It's happening! Your thoughts and emotion are sending the vibration out there and it will be presented. Read it aloud. Believe it! It's Universal. Hold on to it, hold on to it, hold on to it. You're now inventing it. Thought energy, remember. The Universe can't stress enough, the power of thought energy vibration.

I am positive thought energy.
I am positive thought energy.
I am positive thought energy.
I am inspiring others.
I am inspiring others.
I am inspiring others.
I am fit and healthy.
I am fit and healthy.
I am fit and healthy. ***What do you look like? Hold on to it***
I am attracting awesome happenings.
I am attracting awesome happenings.
I am attracting awesome happenings. ***What does that look like, fantasise, smell it, feel it, imagine it***
I am attractive.
I am grateful.
I am happy.
I am wealthy.
I am Universal.

I am happy and love everything! Well, everything you want to be.

I am, I am, I am to anything we want. Positively add emotion to it and hold the fuck onto it. Imagine anything! Add to your list as much as you want. When we imagine what we want to invent, we talk about doing it like it's already happened. With truth is most powerful. Our truth is the love happy thought emotion. This emotion will normally involve other people and is far more powerful when shared as it adds to the thought energy vibration.

We must understand and be conscious of what we are doing if we want to change what we are doing or getting. It's all good shit when we become conscious, and we can start having a fucking great laugh about what we have been doing. This is a game! This whole thing called life is one big game of inventing.

The two words 'I am', are the most powerful words we can ever use. 'I am' describes who we are and how we feel at any point of time, whether we are conscious of it or not. When we use the words 'I am' with truth, everything just rolls as it should, and the Universe is with us.

It's important to be conscious when using the words 'I am'. With enough thought energy emotion behind what we are saying or imagining, we are drawing closer to ourselves and inventing that experience.

"I, I am, I'm". Let's see how many times we catch our selves saying these words today. They are all about 'us' and describe how we feel at that point of time. Even if we think we don't want it, we are making it happen.

KEEP IT POSITIVE

Another few important words to remember. "None, not, don't" are cancelled words. Our subconscious doesn't recognise these words, even when they are added to "I am". None, not and don't mean fuck all to the subconscious when referring to ourselves. Remove them totally from a sentence and that's actually what we are inventing or creating for ourselves. Truth.

BEING AWARE OF - I AM WHAT I AM NOT

> I am a non-drinker
> I am a non-smoker
> I am not fat
> I am not broke
> I am not lonely

Remove not, non and we are all the five things written above. We must be conscious. Think about it. We become, or we are that already, to what we put the words "I am" to. Why would we say what we are not? Put it another way, why would we add emotion to anything we are not already or don't want to be? It is crazy.

We are what we are not, so we must change "I am" to what we want to be. "I am" can be an absolute punish or an absolute gift. It's free will. We get to choose. We are inventing our own lives. We are constantly writing our own movie. Always. We are our thoughts with "I am, I'm, I". We are what we think we are! If we become conscious of what we are telling ourselves, we become what we want.

I AM what I Am, and I am what I am not. We become and invent experiences we put I AM to.

I BECOME WHAT "I AM NOT" WITH I AM

When someone says to us, "don't get angry", our response is often, "I am not angry". We may not in the slightest bit be angry at the time. But if they keep repeating it to us and we keep repeating and replying to them, "I am not angry" we are guaranteed to end up angry if we are not conscious about what we are adding 'I am' to.

Eventually we end up saying, "I am not angry, fuck off, you're annoying me now"! Think about it. We have just said and become, exactly what we said we are not by using the words "I am". Buddha or Jesus for example would never put "I Am", to what they did not consciously want to be. Perhaps it is best to say nothing at all and not even reply. Or allow a bit of space between spoken words.

This doesn't mean we are selfish or arrogant, it just means we know the power of a spoken word, and we are conscious of the bullshit we can easily drag ourselves into and not want to be. Maybe we could just say, "is that right"? We don't even want to hear an answer, but we sure as hell are not going to become what we don't want to be with "is that right".

The words 'I am' can be a beautiful gift. We can easily become anything we want to be.

WHAT AM I?

Someone I love dearly asked me a question a few days ago. "So, who are you"? It was an interesting question and I couldn't really give and answer apart from, "I can't answer that". I didn't really know.

So, later that night when I was back at home I asked the Universe, "Who am I"?

I got told, "Remember the example of what living now

means, about the deciduous tree and reincarnation? There is your answer."

Here it is again in case we have forgotten: Imagine a deciduous tree going through its seasons. When a tree loses all its leaves and looks dead, that's actually when it's at its most alive. We can't see this, as it looks completely dormant to the eye. But all the trees cells are buzzing with energy, creating the buds that will sprout into the leaves and flowers that we will see in six to twelve weeks' time. What we see when a tree is in full bloom was created weeks and months ago. When it looks its most alive, it's actually finished its cycle. Resting and enjoying - you could even call it dying. Well part of it is, it's reincarnating.

Again, reincarnating. We do it every night when we go to sleep, but are not conscious of it. Part of us dies every night and we wake up changed, different every single day.

So, we as humans are no different to trees in nature. The only difference is the tree knows exactly what it's doing, and we as humans mostly have no idea. The tree lives every moment now, and creates every future moment, now. The tree just is and goes with the flow of what it is.

Everything and every future experience is created now. Our thoughts right now are the key to our future and what we want to experience.

Wrap our heads around it! We have caught up to ourselves. The future you is already happening/happened. Yep, it is… but we can change it right now if we want to. If we are happy, don't change a thing. But we must realise that this is all happening now and is always happening now.

We now understand the power of thought energy emotion, truth and mind, and they invent all our past, present and future experiences. Giddy up!

SO, WHO AM I?

When asked that question, "Who are you?" we could answer, "I am in a shit of a mood right now and in my mind, come back and ask me in an hour". It's the mind/ego/brain that is constantly chopping and changing what it wants.

So, who *am* I? If I'm not who I was yesterday - and I am who I am today - but I am not who I will be tomorrow, WHO AM I? I Am LIFE! Forever changing. That's what "I am what I am" means! I am who I am right now this today. Who I am tomorrow has evolved again. Nothing ever stays the same. Woohoo! Yes! How exciting! Evolution.

Ha-ha. It is what it is… LIFE, it's a game. But with truth and love we are giving our true (I am) and not the mind.

We are what we are. We change from day to day. Our thoughts and beliefs on a subject change all the time. How we feel at any point in time – happy or sad, indifferent – changes too. We've all said, "Well that's what I thought at the time, I was wrong". But a thought with love, no judgement, love for someone else's happiness, not ours, can and will invent happy. Because that happiness we give becomes ours. The Universe sees and hears you. With emotion of truth, then everyone's a winner that's the Truth!

You can change whatever you want to invent and experience at any time. Being conscious of what we want and with our Truth is the path to happiness. Truth is Universal remember. Truth is part of God consciousness and we are all part of that.

Universal Connection

Below is an example of our thoughts. Our thoughts move faster than light depending on the emotion behind them. The lines symbolise thought energy from all of us. The stars and dots symbolise a vibrational match. When we are a vibrational match with someone or something, the invented thought is then presented to us in physical life.

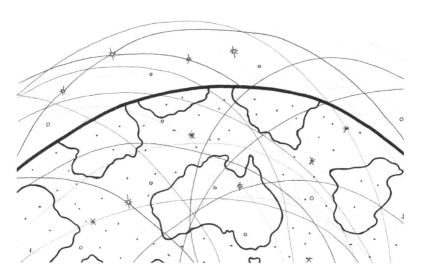

CHAPTER 9

DOES MONEY BUY HAPPY?

There are a million and one books out there on how to become a millionaire, but what does being wealthy really mean? The Universe and I have spoken at length about this. What I got told is a whole book in itself, so I have done my best to break it down.

I asked the Universe about being wealthy, and if it would solve all my problems. This is some of what the Universe told me.

'In the western world, many of you have become confused about money and the happiness it will bring you. Happiness is not bought. Happiness is acquired by you and your soul. It's Universal energy, not a physical thing. What you give. You give happiness and love to others and you create this for yourself. The Universe automatically gives it to you.

Giving people happiness and love could be as simple as a good morning, how are you, a smile, helping someone carry the shopping upstairs, giving some loose change to someone who asks for it.

When you do these things for others, you don't need a thank you. You get that from the Universe already. You feel it when you do it with your truth, you don't need to hear it in words. You sometimes hear people say, "I did this, I did that for so-and-so and they didn't even say thank you". You don't need it, the Universe sees and hears you.

Wanting something is normal. Without want there is no desire and we wouldn't even get out of bed. But wanting for more and more material things can create more unhappiness, more to worry about, and more focusing on what you don't have.

Jake, you wanted money to make your previous partner happy, so she would stick around. Her want for money was so powerful that all you started to care about was the money you didn't have. You spent all your time thinking that you were going to lose her and your family.

And what happened? You got what you thought about. You were both living in your minds. You loved one another dearly, but you didn't focus on that. The love you both were focusing on was more happiness, and the belief that money would bring it.

Your thoughts and conversation about what was happening and what wasn't happening came true. You see, your relationship was based on buying happiness.

You both needed to just stop and realise it was already in front of you. There is nothing wrong with wanting for better or enjoying material possessions, but they do not lead to your happiness. It never ever lasts! Your thought of what money would bring brought you unhappiness. You were inventing with your minds. Your truth would have brought you all the money you ever wanted.

Your minds' thoughts about money brought you incredible pain. But this, in the end, turned out a great thing, remember? That's how you finally got talking to me. What you "thought" was your biggest down, was your biggest up.

Jake, you are now feeling very wealthy, aren't you? You never gave in on life, and she was the last piece of the puzzle that brought you to me, and to receiving this guide. It all happened for a reason, yet you both had no idea. You both needed each other to invent an experience. You wouldn't take all the money in the world for what you have now. You invented it and look what you got to experience. Remember, your down times invent your best. It nearly sounds cruel, but you're doing it.

Sometimes, often, less is more. The more things you have, the more chance you have to create more pain for yourselves. The more you have to lose. The world is becoming very consumed by producing and accumulating more and more material things to make you happy. Material things are a fleeting emotion. A new pair of shoes, a new phone, a new jacket, a new TV, even a fresh hair cut is a fleeting emotion.

It feels good just for now, but disappears very quickly. When you constantly look for happiness in these material things you find yourself always looking for more to feel happy. You cannot buy happiness.

Money is something you all need, and it sure does help with some extra comforts, but happiness will not last from possessions. You need to change your thoughts about money, the whole Universe does.

People make the world continue, not money. Money helps an experience, but money isn't the experience. Your soul doesn't care about money whatsoever. Your culture is becoming more and more conditioned to believing that you need to buy this or buy that to be someone, to stand out, or be anything of value.

Who has made this up? You all have! And most of you are going with the flow that this just is.

Jake, you personally found no lasting happiness from any of these things in the past. You didn't know happy until you got this guide and realised that you are all Universal, inventing your own happiness. Everything else is just an experience, but happiness comes from within, always. Things are things, but true happiness comes from within and sharing it with other people. When you live in the mind you are in that constant horse race that never ends, and you are the only horse in the race. You are at your happiest when you interact with other people or do something nice for another person.

When you are with friends, having a bite to eat and a good laugh. When you are at the beach, when looking at the stars, when holding your beloved partner's hand. That moment then is when you are at your happiest. You are being who you are and living your truth. These emotions are what you call love and have nothing to do with money. It's the simple things, normally the ones that don't require much more effort than "nothing", that you are at your happiest. So, you must ask yourself. You want this money for… why? Is it to take the family on a holiday, or create a comfortable home for them, or to be able to freely give it away? Figure out what it is you want money for. Then, go and get it.

You have a clear path of why you want it, and you already understand your happiness within yourself before you start. Then you will have fun with your money and others will win from you too.

That's as far as it goes, it helps an experience. An experience not shared, normally has no meaning to it. You as a culture are becoming too focused on money and possessions, which are all on loan by the way. Even your body is not yours, it's on loan from the Universe. Most of you seem to think it's yours, but it's not. It's been loaned to you to get around in your physical Universe so you can invent an experience for yourselves.

Your culture is becoming more focused on what you don't need to be more efficient. You are not becoming more advanced as human beings, you are actually going backwards. Working more and living less, to have more. More things and more technology to make life more efficient is actually creating more problems and taking away from your life here. Walking past people and others like they are separate from you and everything is all for one. You are not separate and never have been.

Thinking and acting like it's all about you, it's a mad world and you need to protect "yourself" with money. Doesn't matter about the next-door neighbour or the man or the family down the road that can't afford food, that's their problem right! As long as you're ok. Well, their problem is your problem. Believe it. We are all Universal and one thing creates another that sooner or later becomes a blessing or your problem. None of you are separate, but many of you seem to have forgotten that.

Your culture is making things so efficient that you are "actually" needing more things just to survive. You are creating more things that you don't need that creates another bill that you don't need. You need an iCloud account, you need a Spotify account, you need a Netflix account, you need, you need.

You need to live life that's why you wanted to come here.

You have created a billing system that is so efficient that there doesn't even need to be human interaction anymore. Your computers spit you out a bill to the second. If you don't pay that bill on time you will be sent another bill with interest or a penalty added to it. The human compassion that understands people have problems, is leaving you behind. The computer doesn't care if you have power on in the house or are struggling to eat.

So, you see, if you all keep going this way you are going to *need* to be wealthy. But what of the poorer people who aren't wealthy and can't afford your world's growth? What happens to them? They need to live, so something must give. You are all going to have to give and slow down. You are all in this together. One way or another you are going to find this out if your world keeps going as it's going and keeps forgetting you're not separate. Your world is inventing more and more things you think you need, but you don't. You are making money your world, but most of you can't afford what you think you need. You can't actually keep up with yourselves.

The technology you have now, has you living your lives looking down at a screen, at other people lives that you think are real but are not. It's only a perception. Rather than living your own life, you are day dreaming about other people's lives. But are they even true? You wouldn't know. You have come to Earth because you wanted to invent an experience. Experience with others. You are all missing out on each other. All you must do is look at your public transport in the morning. Jump on a bus or train. Nearly everyone is staring into their phones at mind stimulation. Next to no one is having a conversation, let alone looking up to see what's happening outside.

Jake, what would you say if I told you, sometimes it's as simple as turning to a person beside you and asking them, "how you going, are you good"? You could actually save someone else's life who is living in the mind that day. How much money is that worth? A lot, right. It's immeasurable. Passing the love on, and no money involved. The Universe sees you. If you all did this, you would have all the money you ever wanted.

SO, DOES MONEY MAKE HAPPY?

Money will help if you are happy within already. The Universal Guide is about showing you how to be happy and that is our natural state, to be conscious of what you invent, imagine and wish for. When you get lost in all the outside goings-on and what other people's ideas of happy are, it can be very hard to find your own. All of you can have as much money as you want using thought energy and emotion. It is a good idea to know what it is you are wanting to achieve and just go for it. If its money you want, you can have it. ABSOLUTLEY!

Universal. Everything is connected to the one

Life, a thought

Expect

Expect everything and expect nothing. Then you will have everything.

CHAPTER 10

SO THAT'S HOW YOU MAKE A CAKE

Now we are conscious of what we are inventing. It's not too different to making a cake. A cake needs the right ingredients, mixed the right way, and cooked for the right time to be good. If we make the cake back to front, it will taste shit and turn out looking that way. I was making my life cake back to front for forty or so years. Then, the Universe gave me the ingredients to life, and it changed my life in a split second.

It was like flicking a light on in a dark house. It was instant! Everything we have read to this point is about to come together in one sentence.

We are constantly inventing our lives and physical experiences right now with our thoughts. Right? Right!

I am, even as I write this sentence, inventing everything with my thought energy and emotion. I am inventing more of the past, or I am inventing my different future. You are doing the same as you sit there reading this. You truly are!

It is really a matter of being conscious and aware of what we are doing: it's actually a choice. Yes, *we* are the choice. This is a game. A game we wanted to be in. We call people with luck positive thinkers but there is no luck involved. It's their thought energy inventing that creates their life. They just spend 80% of the time on the positive thought energy line. Not all are conscious that they even do it, they just *are* that thought, or it feels better and that's what they choose to do. Or it's their soul's radar and they go with it.

Remember the 4D hologram projecting our future and what we want? It's as real as the wind and we are doing it right now this very second.

Again, remember right "now", and grab anything that makes you feel good. Imagine anything that brings a smile to your face and hold on to it. Do it with truth and put the love thought emotion, your passion and desire behind it.

Life, a thought

The Illusion

Walk outside during the day and look into the sky. We can't see the stars, but we know they are there. They are just hidden by day for a short while.

Life is this. Slow down, relax and go with the riptide. And remember, what we think we see is often not what is.

Life is a constant show of illusions. The mind can believe all the illusions.

Truth appreciates the illusions as a "show" and laughs at the moon.

I AM MAKING THIS CAKE

So, we now know that we are constantly inventing our own lives and drawing to us the things and people we need to experience. This is it! Imagining, being conscious and aware of what we are inventing. Right here NOW:

<u>I am</u> (whatever it is you want) right <u>now</u> with <u>thought energy</u> <u>emotion</u>.

I Am Now Thought Energy Emotion.

That's what you are inventing. 100 odd pages distilled into one sentence. However, we must practice being aware and conscious of **I AM + NOW + THOUGHT + ENERGY + EMOTION** = us! Our lives, and the future we are inventing right here right now. Those six words (emotions) are inventing our future now, tonight, today, next week and next year. What is it we want to invent, experience, or the people we want to bring into our lives? Imagine it, be it. Even before it physically happens, you are already it the second you imagine it with strong thought energy emotion. If we can feel it and picture it, it's coming. Not giving in is the key. That's the only defining thing.

There is space between our thought inventing and the physical life experience, or that 4D hologram presenting itself in physical form, but you are now inventing it now. The thought energy vibration is being sent out there to the Universe. We just need the passion and to hold on to it. You become it. It's Universal law and the Universal Guide.

That there is how it all works. Really, you say? Yep, that's it! *Universal Guide to Happy* is really quite simple. It's not like digging a hole, it doesn't require physical work – it's largely in our awareness, our consciousness and in our hearts – our truth. All it requires when it comes to physical effort, is getting our ass out of bed. Creating some kind of movement. This minimal movement has required some kind of thought energy whether we are conscious of it or not.

Something as simple as getting out of bed, or even going to the toilet, triggers thought energy, and in turn creates a vibration. It 100% has.

But the real key to consciousness comes through meditation. There is nothing hard about it, it's only practice and it's awesome. This is how we get out of our minds and connect to who we really are. Our soul, the Universe.

REMEMBER AND DRAW ON THIS

I am what I put I AM to.

I am inventing my future right now.

I am inventing my future now with my thought energy

I AM inventing my future **Now** with my **Thought Energy Emotion.** (Passion, desire, love, zest for life, absolute)

Remember this, where you are right now reading this was invented months ago. You reading this right now is actually your past. What a spin out! But it's truth! The future you is already happening or happened. But, you can change it now if you want. Make your own cake NOW! Yep, we can.

Life and any situation we find ourselves in can be changed in a split second with our thought. If it's what you consider negative, see it for what it is, an illusion. I personally look at it as a trial now, of gaining consciousness or "learning" something. A thing only becomes a thing when we label it or put a word to it.

Someone's negative opinion only becomes something if we allow thought to be added to it. What thought do we want to have, or do we just let the vibration fly past, like slipping a jab. Slipping a jab is a boxing term: when someone throws a punch at you, simply move your head to the left or right and let it fly right on past you. Don't get caught by the punch or negative opinion. Slip the jab.

Allowing ourselves to take things personally is also crazy. If we have done something we might think isn't right, we have to take it on the chin. But once we have, let it go straight away. If we live our truth and someone tries to make us feel guilty, let it bounce off. It doesn't belong to us. So many of us are letting our minds and other minds rule our thoughts.

FIND THE SOLUTION – FORWARD MOVEMENT

It's very easy to see someone who is living 80% of their life with truth. If something goes wrong, as we word it, they will quickly get over it. It's happened, and there is no point banging on about it and giving it more life. They will quickly acknowledge that it's happened, perhaps even be a bit pissed off or dismayed, but they find a positive solution moving forward straight away.

Shit happens. How do we move forward to a better feeling? We are inventing it, remember. The Universe always pushes us in the direction we want to go, or what our thought energy vibration is inventing. How often do we look back at what some might call a bad experience, and actually say to ourselves, "thank God that happened"! My whole life has been that, and now I am aware, it was all good.

The Universe showed me this: letting past experiences rule our future is insane. If it does not make us feel good, it must be waved goodbye.

CHAPTER 11

REALISING

The most difficult part of writing this book was trying to condense *Universal Guide to Happy* into a physical entity that we can all easily understand. There is so much to know. If we operated with even 10% of the consciousness available to us, we wouldn't be having this human experience on planet Earth.

Some highly evolved beings, however, are here to guide us. Gurus and prophets such as Jesus, Buddha, Gandhi, Paramahansa Yogananda, Krishna, Mohammed and many more were here on Earth to help us evolve. They were placed here on purpose, to help us remember. You could even say they volunteered.

None of them needed to be here. They were a gift to help us remember. There are similar beings living amongst us now. The Dalai Lama for example, and Paramahansa Yogananda who has since moved on.

ANGELS

Not all angels have wings, and not all angels are dressed in robes. We may not even know when we are face to face with an angel, not by sight anyway. No one is more superior than the other. The soul has no gender or cultural background. It has experienced many and is all. Human conditioning and words have us running anywhere. No different than a dog that loves chasing a ball. Throw a dog 5 balls at once and it has no idea what the hell to do! That's the same as our mind, opinions and conditioning passed on. Otherwise likened to as a shit fight or chaos.

It's great that people inspire us and lift us to another level of wanting to be better and wanting to know more. That's how we evolve. We could liken it to starting school. As we evolve, we go up a grade. But the Universe has billions of different grades that are constantly evolving. It never ever ends for us. No matter how advanced we think we are, know we are not. There's so much truth to Socrates' quote, "the only true wisdom is knowing you know nothing."

Now we can enjoy life. We are in control of nothing but our thoughts. But our thoughts about anything is the gateway to everything. We need to realise how exciting life is! If we are in control of our thoughts, our truth, we are, or are graduating towards, Universal consciousness.

Me, you, all of us are part of the Universe and helping it to evolve. Me, you, all of us have a purpose here on Earth. Every single person, even those that society deems to be the most awful.

Who's to say who is what in the end? That's a human thing, remember. There are some basic guidelines we need to live by, sure, and some don't, and it is what it is. It all comes out in the wash. Why does just about every movie have a villain? Even a children's movie has some kind of villain. Without adversity, there is no triumph. No growth, we don't evolve.

But remember, was that villain conditioned and then living in the mind? There are many villains in movies that come back to the light after remembering their truth and who they really are. An audience may even applaud. What we call real life need be no different.

Life, a thought

My Truth

When the end of the day is better than the start, and the start was freaking awesome! That's how it's meant to be.

Truth, Universal Guide to Happy gave me this. I am it every day now.

Thank you.

JUDGEMENT

Judgement and punishment do not work. Judgement and punishment create more of the same. The minute we are angry we have changed our vibration. The only cure for anger and hate is love. Man-made rules don't work either. No law on Earth can stop anyone from doing anything if they want to do it. Murder, robberies, drugs, whatever, we can go on and on. If rules and laws worked, none of these things would happen.

The only thing that stops anything negative is love. When we realise we are all connected and all part of the Universe, no exception, only then do we graduate.

People who help others for no other reason but to see someone happy for a minute know truth. We all have a purpose.

IT STOPS WHEN WE DECIDE IT DOES

Poverty, hunger, war, racism; God doesn't cause this. Humans choose this. Again, we are separate from nothing and we get to decide if we allow this to keep happening or not. The second we decide it stops, it stops! But it's a collective effort.

Many of us here on Earth blame the Universe when things go wrong. I know I did, constantly! Now, I know I was looking for someone else to blame for my thought energy and my mind inventing.

MY LIFE COMES TOGETHER

I asked the Universe, "Why didn't you help me earlier?"

Universe: Jake, you've loved the surf, swimming, riding motorbikes, being in nature, having a beer with a mate, sex, playing sports, playing with your kids, watching the sun come up, lying in the sun, watching your kids and friends' triumph. You love it! Why?

Me: Because it feels good. Because I'm living, inventing and watching others do that too. Their win feels like mine, and the other stuff just feels good! It's an awesome feeling!

Universe: Why didn't you just ask me to do all that for you then?

Me: I know this is a trick question, but, because I wanted it. I wanted to do, see and feel it. I wanted to know what it feels like for myself. I loved many of the feelings I experienced and wanted more.

Universe: What about your motorcycle accident? Would you want me to take that back from you?

Me: No, it saved my life. I admit I was trying to kill myself without being aware of it. That crash cured my depression that was living hell. I hated my job, and many other things too. It put me on a path I would never want to take back. Truthfully, I know I invented that accident and my life. It just took me another 20 or so years to realise.

Universe: Yes, that's right. And you wanted here on Earth to experience and invent your own movie. And you are getting to do that as you wanted. You are the one deciding if you want to move left or right. At any one second that you choose, you can step to the left or step to the right. You can speak up, or not say a thing. It's your choice. Yours. You get to decide. You even choose when you go to sleep. You close your own eyes when you go to sleep, no one else does it for you. Right?

Me: Yes… here it comes, right? (My truth knew what was coming.)

Universe: So, while all the good things were happening that you invented with your free will, you were happy. The second things didn't go your way, it becomes my fault, not yours, because you thought you and I were separate. And are the 'negative' things ever actually negative?

Jake, at many stages in your life you've loved pain. You

kept on inventing it for yourself. Remember you wanted to be here on Earth. Your motorcycle accident, depression, this made you want for more. Look at the awareness you have now. Look how much you can help others. If I did all this for you, you don't get to invent or feel anything. So, there would be no experience and you wouldn't exist.

The minute you stop inventing, the minute you are no longer vibrating, positive or negative, you are no longer. And you are all, so this will never end. I love you and you know it! Your so-called bad or negative experiences were actually your best! You invented them. So, what does that make your positive inventing and experiences?

I will answer that question for you because I know your answer. There is no win without a loss. There is no positive without a negative, no day without night, less is more, more is less, slower is faster. There is no running race unless someone else is in it with you. You don't even know what fast is unless something else is slower.

All of this is, is. You are me, I am you. I am all that loves you and always will be. You have been getting everything you wanted to experience and invent here on Earth. I have been with you every second of every day. I have wanted to pull up the handbrake on you many times, but what you want, I must allow. Free will. You wanted it. You just forgot till you remembered. Have I made sense to you Jake?

Me: Yes! And for the first time I really know what Amen means.

OK THEN

For me, that was a bit of an eye opener. Love is our truth. It's about being grateful. Everything that we see and every person we meet is a gift. Everything that we can comprehend is part of our life movie. They are all part of the cast to make our movie.

Before I received this guide, I can truthfully say I didn't really know what love was, or what it meant, because I didn't love myself. And if I didn't love myself, how could I receive it from someone else? I was receiving love all the time, but I dismissed it. I didn't realise it was there.

THE LOVE

So, stop right now. There is love. It's you. It's the Universe, God, and who you really are. You are it and when you give some of it away it comes back to you 100-fold. Give it away! Throw it out there like confetti. Honestly, how can that hurt? It cannot! It will only make you feel great. Don't expect anything or a thank you from anyone else, you don't need it. Your thought energy vibration is inventing your life now, it's impossible for it not to happen. The right people and more love than you ever thought possible will come to you.

CHAPTER 12

STUFF WE ALL NEED TO KNOW

I have received so many answers from the Universe to questions on so many different subjects that I couldn't possibly fit them all into one guide. I'm constantly getting more and more answers every day. There is so much to know... but that's a whole other book! In the meantime, here are some good ones the Universe made me aware of.

DEATH AS WE THINK OF IT DOES NOT EXIST

Death is only a word. But we can be very confused about what it actually means. Life is life forever. So, death is also life. Death as we commonly think of the word here on Earth does NOT exist. The physical body expiring just means we've moved on and our soul has moved on from our vision here on Earth.

Our physical bodies are purely on loan from the Universe to invent and experience things here on Earth. When our soul has experienced what it wants, it leaves the body behind, like a caterpillar or snake shedding its skin, or like a tree dropping leaves. It has moved on to more inventing and evolving. The skin now becomes fertiliser for the Earth.

Everything, absolutely everything, is on loan here on Earth. Your body, your car, your house, EVERYTHING! As that big wheel turns around, it's given back, and we move on. The next stage of consciousness you could call it. We are constantly trying to find more ways to live longer here on Earth, but the irony is we live forever already. Do we really want to watch the same movie over and over again?

DO WE GET TO SEE FRIENDS AND FAMILY AGAIN THAT HAVE PASSED ON?

100% absolutely yes! They can see you now. A friend of mine recently told me she thinks she can feel her grandmother with her that has passed on. That's because she can.

Remember, what we see with our eyes is an illusion, only a tiny part of what is actually there and real around us. Think of all the vibrating energy we can't see or sense, all the wavelengths we can measure with instruments, but not with our bodies.

Life is like putting on a pair of virtual reality goggles. Immediately, you're then in the game. But the game isn't real. You know it's not because you can remember who you are. In the game you can even step to the left or right, look around, even lose your balance. When we take off the goggles we say, 'wow, that was so real, it was like I was in it!'

Guess what? You were. Guess what? You are in *this* life game. When we die and move on we just take those goggles (our eyes, our senses) off and realise what a game it has all been. Just a chance to experience a physical life on Earth. We will wet ourselves laughing at how real we thought the Life/

Earth game was, and perhaps even want to come straight back for another go.

Why? To invent what we didn't get to experience the last time around, or to evolve or go to another level. That may be to another planet, to exist at a higher consciousness and evolve even further. It never ends.

In the cosmic world, you get to choose. We get to go backwards or forwards in time, (actually space, because time doesn't exist) or stay where we are. Which is absolute bliss by the way! You can enjoy everything that's being invented from "there" as you are part of it, or you can jump back into the physical game for another crack.

COSMIC TIME

There is no such thing as time. 90 years here on Earth may seem long but in cosmic years, you wouldn't even have time to put the kettle on for a cup of tea. No different to not being able to see the stars during the day, but they're still there and we will see them again as soon as it becomes night. However, it is so much quicker than that. We MUST enjoy this illusion of life while we are here. We wanted it and it's a gift.

THE COSMIC WORLD IS JUST THERE, WE JUST CAN'T SEE IT.

Often in movies we see someone in a police interrogation room. There is always a one-way mirror that they can't see past, or who may be watching on the other side. Here and there is just like that. But on the other side of that mirror is everyone you've ever loved who's passed on watching you and your life game. You will be seeing them again. This is exactly why we can sometimes feel someone who's passed on with us. Because we can. It's their vibrating energy. They are just there. No, they are not watching us in the shower.

Remembering, being aware (which are the foundations of consciousness) lets us see through that one-way mirror. It doesn't have to be with our eyes, it's a knowing. It's Universal. If we all could only remember just how much we wanted to be here! We wanted to come here from the Cosmic world to physically invent and be part of the experience here on Earth.

Live life and don't fear death. It does not exist and we all find this out. That is a Universal promise.

Life, a thought

The peak is the middle

Ask any athlete, or a woman who has given child birth, or someone that's climbed Mt Everest, this truth – It's not so much about reaching the peak, that feeling ends quickly. It's the parts that happen before and after that makes reaching our "peak", mean anything.

DÉJÀ VU

Wow, this is a good one. Déjà vu means you've *done* it before. Yep, you've been here before. What happens though? Do we step to the left or do we step to the right? It's a choice. Our soul has its reasons for being here. We are our souls and we have free will. Whatever we want to invent or change, we can. When it feels good, it's right and we are swimming with the riptide.

When it doesn't feel good and things seem to be hard work, then we are pushing against our soul's purpose and our truth. When it doesn't feel right, we are off track. All we have to do is listen to ourselves. The answer is in us always. That's the Universe trying to pull up the handbrake saying stop! There's a difference between persistence and pushing shit uphill. Stop for a minute. Slow down and sit on this for a second. You've had every single red light put in front of you for a reason. Are you living your mind right now?

When we become aware and conscious, it's actually like getting punched in the chest or slapped across the face. It's suddenly so obvious! It happens to me all the time. I've become aware of the punch and slap. There are still times I don't listen, but they are far less. It's our soul's radar. It always knows, even when we don't. Déjà vu is your cosmic glance into the future. You can also access this state through meditation. When that is mastered, life becomes so much easier.

Meditation isn't about sitting on a rock for hours at a time. It's not putting your body in such a position that all you can feel or concentrate on is the pain in your lower back or if you are breathing correctly. It's about getting out of the mind. Taking those virtual reality goggles off. Being what you naturally are, which is Universal.

I'VE WRITTEN THIS BEFORE

Two years ago, I saw something I read in a dream. I woke up wondering what the hell it meant. Then I forgot about it and never gave it another thought. A few days ago, I had just finished writing a paragraph that is in this guide.

I was reading it back to myself. Then boom I remembered! I've done this before! Son of a B#%#! That's what that meant. Even the room I was in was in my dream. I didn't even live in this apartment back then. Boy did I start laughing, I'd been here before, and wrote this paragraph years ago. What a game I'm in. The best game ever.

HOW THINGS ARE INVENTED

Firstly, we all know that anything invented was once a thought. Secondly, anything ever invented is never to the credit of just one. Anyone who says it is, perhaps isn't living their truth. Anything ever invented is a collective effort. Anything invented is because of a desire for more. Evolution always involves others whether we can see it or not. *Universal Guide to Happy* took 40 years or so of many people coming into and out of my life that gave me an experience that made me want for more. It made me ask the Universe, 'what the hell is going on?'

WHAT IS WORTH FIGHTING FOR?

There is never a fight unless we invent a reason. If we live our truth, there is no fight. The mind wants to fight to justify a right or wrong to itself. To make its opinion right. So, whenever we are so right, we are wrong. We are both, remember?

It has been written that Jesus said, 'turn the other cheek'. I thought it meant that if someone slaps you in the face, turn the other cheek so they could slap that too. That's what we were taught in Catholic school. But I used to think, 'I'm no Jesus, so I'm going to punch you straight back in the mouth twice as hard!'

But this isn't what it means, of course. 'Turn the other cheek' means, slip the jab. Let it go, let it pass you right on by. Do not let people living in their minds and their opinions become part of you. They don't know what they are doing, they are not aware. It doesn't belong to you, so do not let it become part of you. When we live with truth things just slip by us, barely even felt. Our emotion only becomes focused on what we want, not what we don't.

Martin Luther King didn't fight, he spoke his truth with love. There is a big difference. Spreading love is not fighting. It's just spreading love. Gandhi, same thing. Killing in the name of religion is a made-up story by people living in their minds. The Universe would never demand this, it's the opposite to truth. Free will is not dictatorship. So, who made this up? Many minds and opinions of rights and wrongs. Human judgements and passed on conditioning.

We, you, me, everyone, invents everything that happens here on Earth. If something comes to us, sure we need to act. But searching for it when there is another way could be the better choice. We invent what we put passionate thought energy emotion to.

If we are passionate about conflict – think about it, worry about it - we will get it. Being conscious and aware of our truth helps us realise what it is we are actually looking for and what we want to invent. Everyone's end goal is to invent, evolve, give love, be loved and be happy. We just forget.

IS IT ALL ABOUT ME? AM I BEING SELFISH?

Universe: No, it is. Let's call me/us selfish for a second. If I do something good for someone else, it makes me feel good. So, is it about me? No, and it never has been. We are all Universal, so we are all connected. It's never all about me or you. It's about us! We are all in this together helping one another invent and evolve. You feel good because they feel good, and they are you, and you are them. Is it all about me? Yes. And who is that? It's you. And who are you? Them and me. It's really, really simple.

WHAT ABOUT LONELINESS?

Our minds love to make up things that don't exist. But, as we've seen, we can make it our reality by focusing our thought energy emotion on it. 'Look at those people, what are they doing, I'm missing out, why isn't my life like theirs, their family is so normal - why isn't mine, their relationship is perfect, I want that'. Etcetera.

The only thing that is real on Earth is the life we are inventing - our thoughts that we put to anything. And it's not if it's with the mind. We just made the whole thing up.

I have colour blindness. People love to ask me what colours things are. They think it's hilarious because I can't see what they see, and so do I. I play along with the game because it makes me laugh that they are laughing. I love it. I still see colours, heaps of beautiful colours, just not what they see. Colour blindness might be perceived as a deficit but it's not at all. I know no different and I'm not bothered by it whatsoever. I am missing nothing because I don't know any different.

Loneliness is the mind telling you that you must be seeing or doing something because everyone else is and you're missing out. Guess what? They *are* doing something else! There are 8 billion different movies playing, remember?

But their movie is not yours. It is our movie that we have put a thought to, that we think is theirs. Is it true? When we live in the mind we start inventing their life movie for them through ours. We have just totally made something up that is not their truth, or ours.

THE POINT HERE IS, WE ARE NEVER ALONE

When we become conscious, we realise that we are not separate from the Universe/God. We are never alone. When we think we are separate, our minds tell us that we are. When we remember that we are not, we never are. I personally love being around people, but since I've remembered who I am, I am all the time, even when I'm not. You are never alone when you remember who you are. It can be a struggle at times, but know you are never alone. If someone like me can know this, you definitely can!

The Universe, God, is all there is. You are never alone. You are God, part of. We are all connected.

A GAME OF REMEMBERING

Imagine someone you love more than yourself, if that's possible. If someone you love was bitten by a zombie and became one, what would you do? If we live our truth we would try and help them no matter what. We would try and help them remember who they really are. We would understand that the 'zombie' they are, isn't who they really are. We would do anything we could to bring them out of that state.

That's what the Universe is trying to do for us. Trying to help us remember because many of us have become zombies. We need to remember. We are here on Earth because we wanted to be here. When a child leaves home and it's on a path to no happiness, a parent can't say, "don't do this, it will bring unhappiness"! Who's to say which is right or wrong anyway. But a parent never gives in. A parent will find another way to help their child remember and get them back on the path.

Free will? God is a trillion times more than that. God places angels around us all the time to help us remember where home is. Many gurus and prophets such as Paramahansa Yogananda are this. You will know the ones that are angels because they give truth alternatives, not ultimatums. Sometimes it takes a while, and we won't always know who they are just by looking at them.

Remember, we are never alone. NEVER! There is someone that loves us more than we love ourselves, always. Love yourself. Now you are living your truth. Not separate, you are it.

WE ARE NOT RESPONSIBLE

Ha-ha, now that's funny. My motorbike was doing nothing till I decided to make it do something. It doesn't have a soul. It was manufactured by humans and wouldn't move from where it was unless a human made it move.

My motorcycle didn't ride me into my accident, I rode my motorcycle into my accident. When we are separate we like to blame something else. That way, we aren't responsible, and the mind can then wave it off. But the mind never waves anything off, it constantly draws us back in and plays the blame game. This means anything can be used as a weapon to hurt ourselves or others, but it's us that do it, we can be the weapon or our best friend. We are always the ones inventing our life's experiences.

IS TECHNOLOGY REALLY HELPING US?

Universe: Your technology over the last 20 years has exploded. You have advanced by many hundreds of years over the last 20 years. The thing is, you can't handle it. Your consciousness is not advanced, it's still somewhat primitive, and you can't keep up.

For example, take a five-year-old child into a candy shop or toy store and tell them they can have whatever they want. What will you end up with? A sick child from too much candy, or an upset child because there are too many toys to choose from and they don't know what to do with it all. This is where the cultures of your world can help one another catch up. Your West needs your East and your East needs your West. You are not separate, and here to help one another.

Are you advanced, compared to what? You still, as you put it, have third world countries. There is your answer.

WHY ARE THERE DIFFERENT CULTURES AND RACES?

To help us evolve. Different cultures give us different outlooks on life and each one is of equal value. Why do some many of us like traveling so much? Because we get to experience a different way of life. When we do, it improves our quality of life, regardless of what we take away from the experience. Remember, not many of us here on Earth can remember past lives.

We have lived many past lives. We have been many different races. So, when asked what our cultural background is, the only real answer is we are all many. Our colour and body appearance only make up an experience, it's not who we really are. Our soul is free of all labels and classifications. So, judging anyone by the way they look is us in the mind, and a very narrow one at that.

A good Australian friend of mine is of Indian decent. If you were to look at him and make a judgement call from his physical appearance, you would say he is Indian.

The truth is he's as Indian as I am. He was born in Australia and brought up with the Australian culture. He is more Australian than I am when it comes to Australian culture. So, judging a person by how they look, there's the mind right there.

WHY DO WE HAVE A MIND?

To calculate and store things, like a computer, that we need to survive in the physical world. To give physical experience to the five senses. Smell, touch, sight, sound, taste. The mind can have all these senses rule us. When we become conscious, we are in control of the senses.

CONNECTION TO A SOUL MATE

We all have soul mates. I personally know mine. I have known them for many lifetimes. I am connected to this person like no other. I feel when they are happy or sad and I can be miles away from them, even in another country. This person is super connected to my soul. We are one, even when we have tried in the past so hard not to be. But its next to impossible.

But our actual soul mate is us. Remembering our truth is our soul. Your soul is your best mate. Find your soul and you will find your emerged soul mate. Who is it? It's you. You can't make someone your soul mate or wish them to be, they either are, or they are not. They will vibrate to your vibration.

PERSONAL INTIMATE
RELATIONSHIPS – TRUTH IS KEY

In the past when I was attracted to a woman who I wanted to be my partner, I would go into character, not much different to an actor. Most of us have done this at some stage. We try and impress our potential partner and be on our best behaviour. When we start a relationship not living or being our authentic self, it cannot be sustained. It's no different from putting a goat in a suit. Sooner or later that suit becomes stifling hot, and we have to rip it off. It is then our partner says, "I didn't sign up for this", and it all goes south. This works both ways of course. The key to any lasting relationship is by entering it being our truthful self. That is the way forward to lasting happiness.

NEGATIVE THOUGHTS ARE AS
BAD AS CIGARETTES

Yes, this is true. We are all vibrating energy and we are all clear on that now. Every negative thought is felt by the body. We might label it as 'stress' but it's actually just a build-up of negative thoughts. All thoughts are a vibrating energy, so where else do we think the first place our negative vibration would go? It goes to us.

When we cough something up that we must spit out of our mouths, we are getting rid of an unwanted energy. We are not aware, but this is no accident. Sickness more often than not comes from our thoughts. This is our bodies way of getting rid of thoughts that have manifested into our physical bodies.

EVERYTHING IS ENERGY.

However, again the mind loves to blame something else because it thinks it is separate. Truth vibrates at such a level that it eliminates a lot of sickness. Truth recharges the body and has it vibrating at a level that bugs cannot tolerate.

Our thoughts are like the wind shot out into the atmosphere also. When there is a huge build-up of negative thoughts, it is then manifested into the physical. If there is a huge build-up of billions of peoples negative thought vibration in the atmosphere and the Earth, something must give. So here is a thought – where do natural disasters really come from?

FOOD

Tony, a good friend of mine owns a farm just out of Sydney. He's not a farmer, he's a business man. But now days he is on his farm more than he is in the city. I thought I knew what made Tony tick until he invited me to his property one day. Tony is all about Universal energy.

On this particular day I watched him water a small vegetable patch he had grown outside the back of his house. He sat there staring at each vegetable plant he watered. He was at total peace. I watched him and realised what he was doing. He was LOVING every single plant he watered. It was nearly like he was the plant. In actual fact, at that moment in time he was. His vibration was exactly at the same level as the plant he was watering. They were one.

I could feel what he was doing. I could feel his vibration. I walked up to talk to him and see what vegetables he was growing. What I saw amazed me. He had the healthiest-looking vegetables I had ever seen. These were like nothing you would see in a supermarket, these were something special.

Why were his vegetables so big and healthy looking? He

didn't have magic soil, so what was it? It was the love vibration he sent to his vegetables, and they in turn loved his vibration and grew for him. They grew like they did from his love. They are alive like him, part of the Universe like him, not separate, and gave it back.

You see, food grown back as little as 50 years ago was done with thought energy vibration. A farmer needed their food to grow so they could make a living. A farmer naturally loved what they were growing. The care a farmer had to put into their crop was similar to loving a pet. Love it and it grows for you. This is in everything we invent, not just food. It's the vibration we put out there with our thought energy.

One hundred years ago, people ate far less than we do now. Is that because we are bigger now? No. They worked far harder physically than we do now. Nearly everything was labour based. The food had a different energy. Food was grown with love vibration. So, when the food was eaten, it energised them like food is meant to. They wouldn't need more because the vibrational energy of what they ate was more than enough to get them through a whole day.

WHY THEN AND NOT NOW?
WHAT'S CHANGED

So much of what we eat now is manufactured or processed food. When food is mass-produced like this, there is one very important ingredient missing – there's no love vibration. Sure, care is taken in the processing procedure, but there is absolutely no love.

This is why when we eat processed foods we are always hungry and feel unfulfilled. There is a prayer that some say before meal time, "Lord thank you for the food we are about to receive", and so on. But really, most of us actually don't know why we are saying it. My Catholic upbringing told me to say it but didn't tell me why. When we give thanks, it must have emotion behind it, so we send the love vibration. THAT'S what that is about. A spoken word without emotion behind it has little to no power.

If we must eat processed food, we can still send it love vibration and give it the charge it may be missing. Alternatively, eat fresh foods that come from the Earth and have the Universal energy still in them. I'm not a vegetarian but I'm conscious of what energy I want to be eating.

MONEY

I recently spoke to a friend of mine who is very wealthy, wealthy enough to live fifty lifetimes in luxury. I asked him what his secret to making money was. He said, "When I invest in something, whatever it may be, I don't think too much about it. I just expect it to work." He told me that most of the time he had no idea what he was doing and goes with whatever feels right.

He invested two million dollars in a business venture a few years ago and just sold his share for seventeen million. He was laughing about it when he told me. He said, "I had no idea what I was doing when I invested in it, it just felt right, and I always expected it to work. If it didn't it didn't. But I never gave that any thought". The point here being, it doesn't matter if it's one hundred dollars or two million, it's the thought we put behind anything.

I can tell you this man built his wealth purely with his thought energy emotion. This man is Tony. The same man that grows the fantastic vegetables. He only puts thought energy into what he wants and never gives any thought to what he doesn't want. Sure, his life isn't always free flowing, and he does have his challenges like all of us. But his ups are far greater than his downs.

Tony never really sees a down as a down. Some people naturally use the power of positive thought energy without even knowing they are doing it. They just are it because they know they are not separate. Doubt invents doubt, worry creates more worry, and fear brings the things we fear closer to us.

Whenever we need a hand, stop for a minute and ask the Universe for help. You will get your answer.

CHAPTER 13

TUNING IN TO TUNE OUT

Remember, I am no guru or monk and very, very far from perfect. What we talk about here works for me and I want to pass it on. If you have a better way that works for you that's great. We have left this part to the end, but it is probably the most important part to the guide. We are all aware that we are inventing our own lives now, and most of our lives are running off opinions when we are not living our truth.

Meditating is a fantastic way to get out of the mind and connect to the Universe. But if we don't know truth and what we are inventing before we meditate, the effects are only a drop in the ocean to what they could be. And that is the whole ocean. We are separate to nothing, nothing. We are all part of God. The God I know isn't a white man in a robe with a beard holding a cane. If yours is, that's fine.

All we must do is ask ourselves this question. Is the God we picture our 'God', or, is it a picture of past conditionings that we have been told is God? Only our truth matters. Regardless, God is everything and God is Universal.

ONWARDS

Tuning out to tune in can be done anywhere. It doesn't have to be done on a rock with legs crossed. It doesn't have to be done for hours at a time. Five quality minutes can be far more beneficial than three hours spent fidgeting. It's not about how long, it's about how little - meaning, no thought. Emptying out the mind and being left with just *nothing*. That sounds a bit confusing but getting out of the mind requires nothing. This is a bit of a challenge, but its only practice.

Often, we fall asleep during meditation, but the point is to stay awake. I used to fall asleep often. It felt great, and I was out of the mind, so at least I got something right.

IT FEELS GREAT

We have all seen someone in a very deep stare before. A glazed appearance comes over our eyes and we can't really see or hear anything. For that brief few seconds we have no idea what is going on around us. It feels so good we don't want to break the feeling. Yep, you are *there*. This is what focused meditation and tuning into the Universe feels like.

My son once asked me how to meditate and he got it the first time he tried. And we were in a busy outside shopping mall. Lucky little bugger! No luck involved though, remember. When he came out of it, he said, 'Dad, that was awesome, that was the best feeling ever!' He then asked me how long he was doing it for. I told him about two to three minutes. He couldn't believe it. He thought it was only five seconds. That's because in the cosmic world where we are from, there is no such thing as time. He was there, he was where we are all from and what he really is.

START SMALL

Slowing down, appreciating, connecting to the Universe only requires five to ten minutes a day and can be done anywhere. Meditation becomes easier the more its practiced. No different to getting fit, or learning a new skill like an instrument or knitting or shooting hoops. Aim for three minutes the first time, then build up to ten or more.

The reason it's best to start with short bursts is so we can get our minds empty, experience the meditation, and stop before our minds start to butt back in and make us wonder whether it's been 10 minutes yet.

Our minds are so busy that when we try and stop them for a minute, it can take a while to slow them down and empty them out. It's like a meteor that's gathered momentum. The most trying part is pulling up the handbrake on our minds.

GET COMFORTABLE

Get into a comfortable position, sitting upright with our spine straight. A chair is just fine, or the floor or wherever. The reason we want to keep our spine as straight as possible is because our life energy flow and physical connection to the Universe is through the crown of our heads all the way through our spines and into our bodies. Keeping our head up and spine aligned allows the energy to flow.

We are already connected to the Universe, so if we have a disability or are unable to sit up straight, don't worry about it. Get out of your mind and the Universe will look after your flow for you. We are limited only by our minds.

Personally, I can meditate anywhere now. I love being stuck in traffic. It has become my time to tune out. I can even be going for a walk and I can be there. Where is *there*? It's the other side of that one-way mirror we talked about earlier. We are all there and here, we have just forgotten.

But yes, it is most beneficial to meditate somewhere quiet and relaxed.

WHEN IS THE BEST TIME TO MEDITATE?

Personally, I find the best time is first thing in the morning, before our minds get hold of us. Got to do this, got to do that, I'm late for work and so on. I love to do it super early, which for me is around 5am. There are minimal distractions, and usually everyone else is still sleeping.

Our thoughts are vibrating energy shot out into the Universe. Many of us live in busy cities with millions of people. If everyone else is asleep, all that thought energy vibration is clear of me. The vibrations of sounds, radios, and others thoughts are very low and peaceful, and so, the atmosphere I am in is that.

If we are not waking up in nature and if we live in a busy city, trying to meditate when everyone else is up and thought vibrations are flying around everywhere can make meditating or tuning out more of a challenge. We are all connected, remember.

SLOWING DOWN

When first learning to meditate or get out of the mind the simplest way can be by just holding a rock, or a leaf. Close your eyes and feel it. What does it feel like, rough, smooth, cold, heavy? Pretend it is you. Close your eyes for three to five minutes and pretend you are it. Then, start listening for all the different sounds you can hear. Move beyond background noise like the TV, and listen for whatever is happening in your surrounding environment. – animal noises, someone speaking further away, a car horn, the wind picking up. This starts to train us how to get out of our minds. Doing absolutely nothing is far more difficult than we think.

GETTING READY TO TUNE OUT

Getting the body ready for Universal energy flow helps us prepare for meditation. Many people find gentle, calming music effective to get into a relaxed state.

Then we start at the left side of our face. Tense the left side of the face for 6 seconds then relax. As we tense each part of our bodies, breathe in for 6 seconds and out for 6 on the relax. Breathe everything out on the out breath. The 6 seconds doesn't matter so much. Just guess.

Tense the left side of the neck and shoulder for 6 seconds, then relax. Tense the left arm and hand for 6 seconds, relax. Left quad, left calf, left foot. Then, at your feet, switch across to the right side of your body and come back up. Right foot, right calf, right quad, right arm and hand, shoulder and neck, and face.

When you get to your head, give yourself a head massage with your fingers. This is self-love and always puts a smile on my face.

UNIVERSAL LIFE FORCE – THIRD EYE COSMIC GLANCE

It's said in meditation that the breath is one of the most important things. This is true in part. Breath/oxygen is energy. But focusing on our breath is actually taking us out of our minds. It's said that when the guru Paramahansa Yogananda was in deep meditation, you couldn't even hear or see him breathing, and his heart was nearly at a standstill. His body was here, but he was there. Focusing on breathing helps take the mind away from over thinking, such as what we are having for dinner, or what so and so said when we did this that and the other. We leave physical Earth when we are in deep meditation.

Breathing is the first step to tuning in. Breathe in a full deep breath for 6 seconds, hold in for 6, and all out for 6. Repeat as many times as needed until you feel relaxed or a little light headed. Meditation is a cosmic drug, and it's so good.

Once we are relaxed, breathe in whatever way feels right for you. This requires no effort and no thought. Go back to focusing on breathing if your thoughts start to wander.

Ok, so now we are *being*. We are connected to the Universe from our crown. Cosmic energy flowing through our heads all the way up and down our spines. You may be able to feel this on your first go or it may take a little practice.

Then, we focus on our Third Eye, or spiritual eye as it's called. This is between our eyes slightly above the brow.

Here we may or may not see a light or eye shaped light. This is the spiritual eye. Here is where we focus on being grateful and being part of the Universe. Look into and through it, like looking into a telescope. When we look through it, it keeps opening up on itself. It's never ending, and you will know. You become one with it all. It is the most peaceful loving feeling you will ever experience. Sometimes it gets so much it can take your breath away, or when you open your eyes you can feel dizzy or like you are on drugs for a while. The cosmic drug. This is God, and Universal is part of who we are.

In this cosmic glance, you can ask pretty much any question you need an answer to on any decision you are wanting to make, and you will get an answer. Maybe not that second, but it will come. You can thank the Universe and remember who you are. You can send anyone you want love when you are there, and they WILL receive it. The cosmic/ spiritual eye is love. Love is truth. The fastest way to truth is through meditating.

Universal Life Force

Universal connection and souls life force

Third Eye, Cosmic glance

This is normally acquired through meditation. Also known as our 3rd eye. Look through it like a telescope. Lean into it like you are leaning into a strong wind and watch it open up.

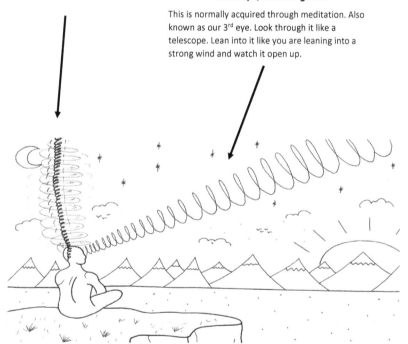

The end is the start

During the day we can't see the stars because of the light from the sun. The stars are still there but we can't see them with our eyes. Light has blocked out the dark. Night is also light. Night gives us the opportunity to self-realise and to go within ourselves and see light inside us without the distractions of the day. The stars are inside us always, otherwise known as God.

What we can't see is more real than what we can. Love plus thought energy is all there is. Love for each other and allowing others to be as they are. If we want to change something, change ourselves. Change our thoughts to love and there is happiness. It's all there is. The rest is just stuff.

Sometimes, we need to just slow down. Stop freaking out and constantly looking elsewhere. It's in us already, always has been.

So, hello God, to all of you. Yes! You are it, part of. You are the truth, *The Universal Guide to Happy*. It has always been you.

The End – but the end is the start

Universal. Everything is connected to the one

Words used in this Guide and their best meanings.

Anger, worry and hate	Make us feel terrible. That then becomes our vibrating energy. To hate anything requires us to think about it. A powerful thought with emotion invents more of the same. The only thing more powerful that cancels these emotions, is Truth, which is love.
Consciousness/ Awareness	Our connection to the Universe/ God. It's not a physical thing. It's everything that is and who we naturally are, and that equals peace and happiness. Being aware develops our consciousness, and that keeps on growing.

Emotion   Emotion is a feeling about a thought, positive or negative in our mind or truth at the time. **Motion** is absolute movement of energy. Whether we can see it moving such as a car driving down the street, or invisible such as wind and sound. Some motion you can see, other motion/energy you can't see, but it's there. What we can't see with our eyes physically, exist more than what we can see. Emotion voiced and held onto for a long enough time with passion, creates every single circumstance in our life.

Mind   Ego, anger, fear, worry, hate, judgement, disappointment, pain, sorrow, blame. The mind is like being the only horse in a race that never ends. The mind is constantly lying to us and who we 'think' we are is not who we really are. Otherwise known as ego. Our mind is always lurking around. Free will allows us to pick, mind or truth. Mind is part of the brain. The brain is basically an advanced computer and fantastic storage unit that helps calculate things through our senses. But like a computer, the brain is constantly getting viruses. Believing everything we see and hear is not our Truth.

Now   The past, present and future happens
               now this second. Truth or mind +
               thought + strong emotion combined
               now to bring anything we can dream
               of to life. Otherwise known as
               burning desire, or passion.

Passion   Invents life experience. It's done with
               mind or truth.

Thought   Without thought nothing in this
               Universe would have been invented or
               exist. But thought, without emotion
               stops. Emotion is what brings a
               thought to life and into the physical
               experience. The power of thought
               is one of life's most important and
               powerful inventions.

Truth   Love, consciousness, awareness,
               happiness, passion, openness, lack of
               judgment, soul's journey, forgiveness,
               compassion, our personal radar. Love
               for everyone, or even our favourite
               hobbies like playing an instrument.
               Truth is the only consistent emotion
               that ever feels good.

Universal	God and all of us. We are all a collection of God, and anything we think that isn't, is as well.
Vibration	Everything is a vibrating energy. Every thought, colour, thing, sound.
Words	A spoken word with emotion has massive energy vibration. Whenever you try to explain an emotion with words, the experience can be incredibly difficult to get across. If we haven't experienced surfing, sex or childbirth, words can't explain exactly the emotion of it.

FURTHER READING

Anyone who wants to know the ancient teachings of meditation that are proven to work. If you wish, you can sign up to Kriya Yoga meditation (Paramahansa Yogananda). This is an advanced method, with a step-by-step guide to knowing your true self through meditation.

Lightning Source UK Ltd.
Milton Keynes UK
UKHW010631021121
393250UK00002B/249

9 781504 315104